D0987292

KATY'S BABY

KATY'S BABY

THE STORY OF DENISON TEXAS

By Jack Maguire

NORTEX PRESS ★ Austin, Texas

FIRST EDITION

Published in the United States of America
By Nortex Press
An Imprint of Sunbelt Media, Inc.
P.O. Drawer 90159 ★ Austin, TX 78709-0159

ISBN 0-89015-847-9

Additional copies of this book may be ordered by sending $22.95 to the following address:

DENISON PUBLIC LIBRARY
300 W. Gandy
Denison, TX 75020

Dedicated to Claud Easterly,

retired editor of the *Denison Herald,* who knows Denison better, and who has written more about it, than any living individual

Contents

A Personal Note

This book has been fifty-three years in the writing.

It began when I was a very young grade school student at Peabody School. Dr. Alex W. Acheson, A. H. Coffin and other of those stalwarts who had been there when Denison was founded were still alive. They generously acceded to my childlike request for interviews, and I still have my notes from these sessions.

In 1938, barely out of Denison High School, I wrote my first book. It was *A Short History of Denison, Texas,* and it was based largely on those interviews. Published by Ed and Roy Miller at their F. W. Miller Printing Co., it was a kind of local best-seller. The only printing of 1,000 copies was snapped up at twenty-five cents per book.

It was then that I made a pledge to myself that one day I would write the story of Denison as I felt it should be told — not as a dry, dull history, but in human interest terms. This is that book.

To put the story of Katy's baby on paper, I had to prove Thomas Wolfe wrong. He said you can't go home again. You can if home is where you were born, grew up, graduated from high school, held your first newspaper job and met Ann Roddy, the girl you would one day marry.

Coming back home isn't easy. For those of us who left so long ago, there is a sense of loss and heartache on returning and remembering things as they used to be. Both of my old schools are gone — Peabody, converted into administrative offices, and old Denison High, vacant with windows boarded and its ground unkempt, a derelect that once was a Main Street landmark.

And Main Street is now a shadow of the vital commercial artery it was when I left Denison in 1945. I miss the theaters — especially the Rialto and its "bank nights" — and Madden's and Kingston's Drug and Dad & Lad's, where I once clerked. And the White Pig and the Tom-Tom, where every courting couple stopped at least once on every date.

Most of all, I miss the sounds and the smells of the Katy. I especially miss being awakened long after midnight by the wail of the steam locomotive whistle as No. 4, the *Katy Limited,* steamed up the hill from Bona Junction past the Eisenhower birthplace and into Union Station.

I wonder sometimes what would have happened if I had stayed in Denison. I'm sure that Ann and I would have loved it even more than we do as expatriates. When we lived in Denison, we thought it was the greatest place in the world. Despite the changes, we still do. That's the message I hope the story of Katy's baby leaves with the reader.

Acknowledgments

Although I have boldly signed my name as author, this book really is a community effort. Many individuals, organizations and groups have contributed to it.

The Munson Foundation, created by the family that helped found the town in 1872, made the book possible by providing a generous grant. The Denison Public Library, that cultural gem which is the envy of other Texas cities of comparable size, will benefit from the sales. Alvin Bailey, director of the library, Dixie Foster and other members of the staff made their facilities available, provided research help and offered encouragement.

Ann Roddy Maguire, the wife I met when we were students at Denison High School, should share equal credit for this book. A writer and editor in her own right, she spent long hours helping with research, editing and re-editing the final draft of the manuscript, working with the publisher in designing the book, selecting the illustrations and seeing it through final production.

Claud Easterly, the retired editor of the *Denison Herald*, who gave Ann and me our first newspaper jobs and who has been our mentor and friend for half a century, was an invaluable contributor to this volume. He opened his personal files to us, is the photographer responsible for many of the pictures and is the individual who spent long days editing the original manuscript and making suggestions. The book is dedicated to him.

Donna Hunt, present editor of the *Herald* and author of many articles on Denison's history, provided background material, photographs and guidance. My old friend of many years, Mayor Ben Munson IV, enthusiastically supported the project at every stage. C. J. McManus, for whom I once worked in his Dad and Lad's Store and who has done so much to renovate Main Street and save Union Station for posterity, gave us access to his personal files and helped in uncounted ways. So did his secretary, Louise Blanton.

My high school classmate, Keith Hubbard, and his wife, Jo, gave moral support and encouragement. Another old friend, Ralph Douglas, and his wife, Lamoyan, spent hours checking historical records and selecting photographs from their own collection. Paul Horn of Dallas and Mrs. Pete Mannery helped us establish the fact that the house at 1524 West Crawford probably is the oldest residence in town still serving as a home.

Among those furnishing photos and information were Clara "Kedda" Heimburger Rienzi of Dallas, Julia Johanning of Las Vegas, Nevada, Congressman Lamar Smith of San Antonio and Washington, D.C., Floyd and Helen Everheart of Sherman, and David O. Bear of Jackson, Mississippi. Louis Pollaro of Pollaro Productions gave us photographs and took time to discuss with us his concept for making Main a "theme street."

W. David Bayless, Sr., provided pictures and facts on the efforts to make Main Street a pedestrian mall. Britt Swain loaned valuable old historical materials. Peggy Roberson of Pottsboro, the artist whose murals adorn several Main Street buildings, supplied information about her work. Former Mayor Bobby Cherry offered invaluable help, as did Bill Cockrell of Dallas and Omar Briggs.

Anna McKinney, Chamber of Commerce tourism director, provided a remarkable collection of historic photographs. So did Jim O'Brien of the Union Station Railroad Museum and H. C. Dulaney, curator of the Sam Rayburn Library and Museum in Bonham. Vicki Hempkins at the Frontier Village Museum in Loy Park loaned photographs and valuable research material.

City Councilwoman Lee Alyce McGrew, a descendant of one of the holders of the original land grant where Denison is located, supplied pertinent information. So did Dixie Edwards Klein of New Braunfels, who sent background material and the photograph of her father and his famous bugle.

Robert C. Stevens of Pittsford, New York, the great-great-grandson of Robert S. Stevens, general manager of the Katy who built the line into Denison and had the townsite laid out in 1872, provided family history and photographs.

Dr. James Denison Briggs of Kerrville, a descendant of George Denison for whom the city is named, furnished genealogical data on that family. Peggy Bevan Vaughan loaned her scrapbooks and many valuable photographs. Fire Chief Bill Taylor provided photographs, as did Postmaster James Hammons. Thelma Braun loaned many clippings and illustrations.

The book is enhanced by the excellent historical drawings by the late Rev. H. Daniel Morgan, former pastor of the First Christian Church. Dr. Morgan made the drawings to illustrate his book, *The Early Days of Denison and The Story of Our Church*, published in 1961. Some are reproduced here with permission of the Morgan family and the First Christian Church.

Peggy Wedding, who knows the town so well, shared information and loaned historical materials.

I regret that there are dozens of others whom I can't thank here or in person. They are the city officials, the business leaders, the Katy Railroad employees and so many individuals whom I have known over a lifetime. Memories of them are a part of this book.

To all of these (and many that I probably have unintentionally omitted), I am indebted for helping to make this book theirs as well as mine.

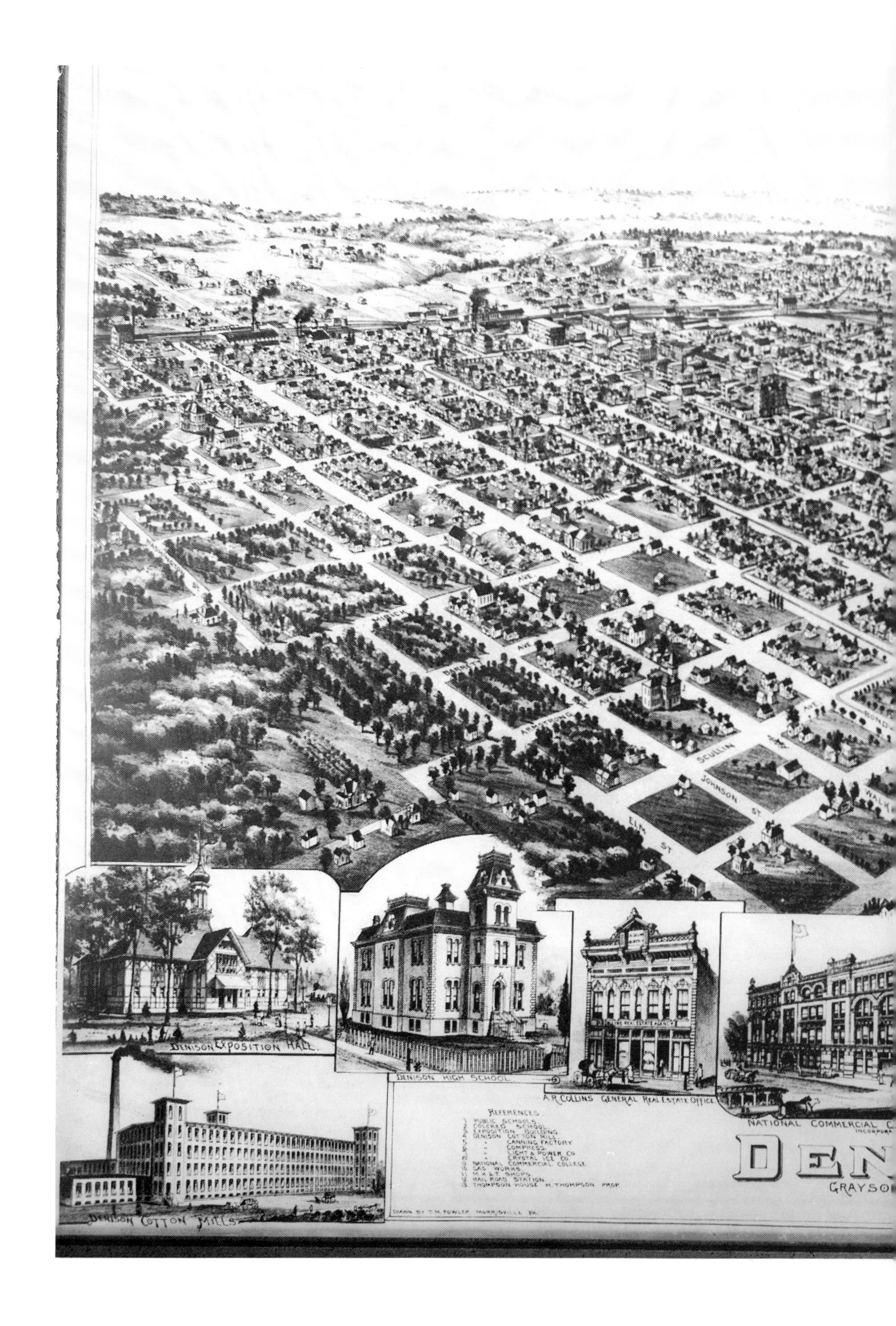
ELM ST
JOHNSON ST
SCULLIN
ARMSTRONG
DENISON EXPOSITION HALL
DENISON HIGH SCHOOL
A.R. COLLINS GENERAL REAL ESTATE OFFICE
REFERENCES.
1 PUBLIC SCHOOLS.
2 COLORED SCHOOL.
3 EXPOSITION BUILDING.
4 DENISON COTTON MILL.
5 " CANNING FACTORY
6 " COMPRESS.
7 " LIGHT & POWER CO
8 " CRYSTAL ICE CO
9 NATIONAL COMMERCIAL COLLEGE.
10 GAS WORKS.
11 M.K.&T. SHOPS.
12 RAILROAD STATION.
13 THOMPSON HOUSE H. THOMPSON PROP.
DRAWN BY T.M. FOWLER MORRISVILLE PA.
DENISON COTTON MILLS

CHANDLER
MORTON ST.
PERRY
EDDY
AVE.
SEARS
ST.
GANDY
ST.
BROWN
WOODARD
MAIN ST.
CHESTNUT ST.
C.S. COBB PRES. H.S. ERNST CASHIER B.D. FISHER VICE PRES.
"THE NATIONAL BANK OF DENISON"
DIRECTORS
THE STATE NATIONAL BANK OF DENISON TEXAS.
CAPITAL $100,000.00 SURPLUS & PROFITS $40,000.00
ISON TEXAS.
SON,
TEXAS
A. ST PATRICK'S R. CATHOLIC CHURCH.
B. BAPTIST
C. CHRISTIAN
D. ST LUKES EPISCOPAL
E. GERMAN EVANGELICAL
F. FIRST M.E.
G. M.E. SOUTH
H. FIRST PRESBYTERIAN
CONGREGATIONAL
A.M.E. CH.
M.E. CHAPEL
BAPTIST
COLORED DENOMINATIONS.
PUBLISHED BY T.M. FOWLER — JAMES B. MOYER

1

The Infant Wonder

"What makes a city? Not houses finely rooted or the stones of walls well-builded . . . but men able to use their opportunity."

— Alcaeus (611–580 B.C.)

A New York journalist, visiting Denison shortly after its founding on September 23, 1872, called it "The Infant Wonder." A better nickname would be "Katy's Baby" because it is the child of the Missouri-Kansas-Texas Railroad.

Since 1870, when the MKT split from the Union Pacific, Southern Branch, and assumed the name Missouri, Kansas & Texas Railway, it had been known as the KT. This euphonious acronym soon became "Katy."

Denison, named for George Denison, a vice-president of the road, was not the only townsite created as progeny of the line as it built toward Texas. Denison, however, became its principal offspring.

If Denison is, indeed, "Katy's baby," its birth might never have happened without the mid-wifery of Benjamin Franklin Colbert, a half-breed Chickasaw Indian, who was gifted with shrewd financial acumen. He was the right man at the right place when the railroad's labor pains demanded that a new town be born in Texas.

Colbert, son of a Chickasaw chief and a French mother, left his tribal home in Mississippi in the 1840's to relocate in Indian Territory. In 1853, he had received permission from the Tribal Commission to establish a ferry to haul passengers and freight between the Territory and Texas. The business prospered and in the mid-1850's he and some partners had set up a store on the Texas side of the river to serve his ferry traffic. He called it the "First Chance, Last Chance."

Colbert's store was the beginning of a settlement that became known as Red River City. Its exact location is unknown, but it is thought to have been north of Duck Creek and east of the present U.S. Highway 75. Supposedly it was about 200 yards from the ferry dock, which would place it near where the old toll bridge stood. When the Butterfield Overland Mail and Stage began service to Texas in September 1858, Red River City became an important stop and a growing settlement. (Sand Springs, on the southwestern edge of Denison, also was a site where the stages paused for a refreshing drink.)

Meanwhile, the Houston & Texas Central Railroad building from the south, and the Katy from the north, were planning a terminal in Texas. Red River City seemed the logical place for one or the other. It was a bustling but raucous frontier town. One writer said it had no citizens, but that its saloons and dance hall were peopled with "denizens." (He intended that perfectly good term to be derogatory.)

At best, its population was mostly transient — wagon masters and their riders waiting with their long trains to cross the river on Colbert's Ferry, and cowboys with their herds that rested overnight there. For all, it was the last opportunity for a binge before heading across Indian Territory to the Kansas railheads.

Sherman or Bust!

Although it seemed the likely stopping point for the Central road, Red River City had been ignored by the Katy surveyors routing their line into Texas. Actually the Katy had never planned to build its own railhead. Sherman, established when Grayson County was organized in 1846, already was a thriving town. It was expected to welcome a railroad that would provide service to St. Louis.

In 1872, when this photo was made, Denison had more tents on Main Street than it had wooden buildings.
— *Author's Collection*

Katy officials were confident this was true because General Manager Robert S. Stevens had come to know a young Sherman entrepreneur named William Benjamin Munson. Born in Fulton, Illinois, and an engineering graduate of the University of Kentucky, Munson and two of his brothers had migrated to Texas. They picked Sherman as a base because it seemed destined to become the queen city of the Red River Valley.

When young Munson and Stevens met, they liked each other immediately. The Katy general manager told the young businessman frankly that he wanted Sherman as the railroad's Texas terminal, and Munson agreed to take the lead in getting the city's financial backing.

However, the H&TC, the Katy's rival, was building north from Dallas planning to continue through Sherman and terminate at Red River City. As the rails neared the county seat, however, it appeared more and more likely that this would be the terminus. Since Sherman was confident that it would be the end of line for the H&TC, there was little support for a second railroad. The town council rejected Munson's proposal to issue the $50,000 bonds needed to get the Katy.

At the time, this was a great disappointment both to Robert S. Stevens and to Ben Munson. However, it turned out to be a bonanza for the new town the Katy would now be forced to spawn, because Munson responded by throwing in his lot with the railroad. Not only did Munson aid the MK&T in acquiring land for the townsite, including property of his own, but he moved to the new town and became one of its most prominent citizens and civic leaders. In fact, his involvement with the town from its beginning until his death was so great that many still think that Munson would be a more appropriate name for it than Denison.

Munson realized that Sherman's failure to welcome the Katy left the road in a quandary. Both he and Stevens recognized Red River City as the next best site for their terminal, as had the rival H&TC. That road already had surveyed its line beyond Sherman, acquired the needed right-of-way and was hoping to get its rails to Red River City before the Katy.

The Katy's other option was to persuade the H&TC to let it share Red River City and exchange freight there. However, this would require the Central to assume with the Katy the cost of a bridge over the Red River. The Texas road refused.

The Katy had only two alternatives — either to stop at the Red River or to build its own bridge and then acquire, lay out and build its own townsite. It chose the latter.

Building the railroad from the river to the possible townsite four miles south of the river wouldn't be easy. The H&TC surveyors, arriving first on the scene, had chosen the best, most level land on which to build the least expensive line. This left the Katy facing topography on the Texas side that offered barriers, such as hills and Duck Creek, that had to be crossed. This spelled more costly construction — and the Katy was almost bankrupt.

The Indian Who Found the "Trail"

Enter "Chickasaw Ben" Colbert. He was neither an engineer nor a surveyor, but his Indian heritage gave him a unique knowledge of land. He also had learned how to turn a fast buck. He combined both talents to benefit the Katy.

Colbert knew every inch of the land between his ferry and Sherman. Riding horseback and using only his eyes to sight the terrain, he examined each valley, hill and ravine and charted an easy route from the river along the level prairie. He was so confident in his judgment that he rode on to Sherman and paid $4,000 in gold for the land that he knew had to be the best possible route for the railroad.

It was a sizeable gamble for an uneducated Indian who had arrived on the banks of the Red River with a total capital of 50 cents in cash and three black slaves! His wealth had come from his knowledge of the land, and he had guessed right again. Katy engineers agreed that he had found the right-of-way that was almost, but not quite, perfect.

Although Duck Creek was the only stream of any size that had to be crossed, even Colbert's route could not escape entirely the steep grade up from the river bottom. It would always be one of the more troublesome grades on the system to negotiate. Until the introduction of powerful diesel locomotives in the 1940's, long freight trains had to be helped up the Red River Hill by an additional "pusher" engine. Known in railroad parlance as "hill engines," these small switchers were a regular assignment for crews.

Despite this problem, Colbert's route made it feasible for the Katy to continue laying track south through Indian Territory to the river. After O. B. Gunn, the railroad's chief engineer, gave his approval, a townsite in Texas had to be chosen. In the early summer of 1872, Gunn decided exactly where he wanted the last spike driven and a station built.

Now the problem was to keep land prices from skyrocketing. Both Gunn and General Manager Stevens knew that once it became known that a new town was in the making, land costs would soar.

Ben Munson would see that they didn't. Working behind the scenes with Robert S. Stevens and other Katy officials, Munson took on the task of buying this valuable real estate while not arousing suspicion. Without revealing their purpose, the two friends immediately began getting title to the land they would need for their townsite. The original plat by Major George Walker of the Katy's engineering staff covered only 393 acres. However, Munson and Stevens bought thousands of adjoining acres for themselves, confident that Denison would grow.

Although scrupulously honest in their transactions, neither hesitated to use a ruse to accomplish their goal. In one instance, Augustus A. Smith, the father of Robert S. Stevens' wife, Mary, was visiting in Sherman. They induced him to pose as a breeder of fine stock interested in establishing a ranch in North Texas so the sellers wouldn't suspect that the

Katy's first passenger and freight station in Denison, 1872.
— *Jenkins Studio*

railroad was involved. Similar parcels were picked by others acting for Munson and Stevens.

They bought much of the land for $20 an acre, which was fair market price at the time. Before they acquired all they wanted, however, word got around that something big was in the making. To get the last two small tracts they believed vital to their townsite — one of 62 acres, the other of 50 — they had to pay $50 per acre. That was a price considered outrageous at the time, but the two entrepreneurs knew it was worth the cost.

The principal tract selected for the townsite, the area that comprises the heart of the city, was that of W. R. Caruthers. Another 3,000-acre tract belonged to Ramon Rubio, a veteran of the Texas War for Independence. (One of his descendants, Lee Alyce McGrew, is a Denison resident and was a member of the City Council in 1991.) Much of the Katy's right-of-way north to the Red River is on the original Rubio land grant.

Stevens didn't delay in getting lots ready for buyers. He dispatched a crew to survey the site. One member was Arthur H. Coffin, whose father, A. V. Coffin, was one of the signers of the original MK&T charter. The surveyor-son is credited with the gridiron design and wide streets that mark the older section of the city.

Unlike most of the Katy executives and workers who returned to their homes once the last spike was driven, Coffin liked the new town and stayed on. He served several terms as tax assessor-collector, worked as a bank bookkeeper, sold insurance and real estate and remained active in Denison until he was in his eighties. (The author still has his notes from interviews with Coffin in 1936–37 — notes that have helped to add much color to the early history of the town nobody really wanted.)

Once Coffin finished the town plat, Stevens sent it to George Denison, the Katy vice-president who was running the railroad while Levi Parsons, the president, was in Europe trying to peddle bonds to finance construction. Although Stevens now owned the entire townsite, the name he put on the plat was "Denison." This premeditated act of flat-

Robert S. Stevens, the Katy Railroad general manager, who founded the new town in Texas.
— *Robert C. Stevens, Pittsford, NY*

George Denison, who never saw the town that bears his name.

tery brought immediate approval from the railroad's chief executive, and the word would proceed.

The Little Bit of England That Is Denison

The name "Denison" is as British as a bowler hat or a pint of bitters. It is an ancient English surname, "the son of Denis." However, William Haynes, expert on the Denison family genealogy, suggests that it may almost be as old as recorded history.

Since Denis was the patron saint of France, Haynes suggests that the first English Denison may have landed with William the Conqueror in 1066. However, the Danish version, Denisca, appears in the old Anglo-Saxon Hundred Rolls. Whether the original Denison was a Norman soldier or a Danish pirate, one of his descendants was destined to establish the family in America. His name was George, and he was a direct ancestor of the man who would give his name to a new town in Texas.

The George Denison of 1872 was hardly the ordinary founding father of a Texas town. He was not a Texan. He had neither lived in the state nor had any connection with it. In fact, there is no record of his ever having even visited the town named for him.

Who, then, was George Denison?

Not much biographical data exists. The original George Denison, a British cavalry officer, arrived in Massachusetts in 1631 — only eleven years after the Pilgrims. He established a family dynasty that would give many pioneers and leaders to this country. However, the man whose name Katy's town bears apparently had few aspirations beyond making money.

In *The Katy Railroad and the Last Frontier,* a fascinating history of the road by V. V. (Scotty) Masterson (1952: University of Oklahoma Press, Norman), Masterson describes Denison, the man, this way:

"He was not a railroad man, not an empire builder. By present-day standards, he was a buccaneer, operating on the fringes of legitimately organized business."

Born in 1822 in Colrain, Massachusetts, he was fifty when the town was named for him. Masterson describes him as "big and stoutish, florid and given to outbursts of choleric temper." Denison had no close friends, but he had money and power — and these got him a place on the Katy's board of directors.

George Denison was never much in the headlines, but he gained some prominence when President Lincoln appointed him controller of the Bureau of Customs in New York. Masterson writes that soon there were strange rumors of merchant ships that were circumventing the blockade of various ports by sailing under two colors. In Southern waters, they flew the Confederate flag and produced papers showing they were trying to run the Union blockade. In Northern waters, they flew the Stars and Stripes and carried credentials showing they were running the Confederate blockade.

This shipping activity was highly profitable, and rumor had it that Commodore Vanderbilt was the brain behind the scheme. Investigation, however, revealed that the ships were all registered in the name of a George Denison. It was never proved that he was the same Denison who was working as controller of customs.

Later Denison took the same job at the Port of

When John Scullin and his track layers crossed the Red River, they achieved Robert Stevens' goal of having the Katy reach Texas at last.

— *Drawing by H. D. Morgan*

S. A. Cook, who purchased the first lot on September 23, 1872, for $250.
— *Ralph Douglas Collection*

New Orleans. Again mysterious things started happening. Masterson writes:

"Valuable cargoes of cotton and other materials cleared mysteriously from 'hither to yon' and back again, until eventually a suspicious admiral . . . began to make inquiries. Strings were pulled, however; power came from somewhere to stifle the investigation and war's end made it pointless."

Through it all, Denison said nothing. He died on February 15, 1876, in Washington at age fifty-four. By then, the town named for him had become a growing railroad center.

Four years earlier, Denison had completed his Federal service and was representing Eastern investors on the Katy's board when Coffin completed his survey. Townsite lots were hurriedly made ready for sale by the late summer of 1872 because railroad management was impatient to get the town established. They hoped it could be done without any more opposition from Sherman interests. They were wrong.

Sherman Starts a War

Newspapers in the county seat began devoting columns to derisive editorials claiming that the railroad was bankrupt, that it had no charter and could never enter Texas legally. Even if these problems could be solved, the editors claimed that the town the Katy hoped to create would never amount to anything. In a final diversion, Sherman residents petitioned the district court to issue a restraining order stopping all construction on the railroad. Still another group organized the early settlers to oppose the sale of any lots in the new town except at nominal prices.

Nevertheless, on September 23, 1872 — the day the Denison Town Company auctioned the

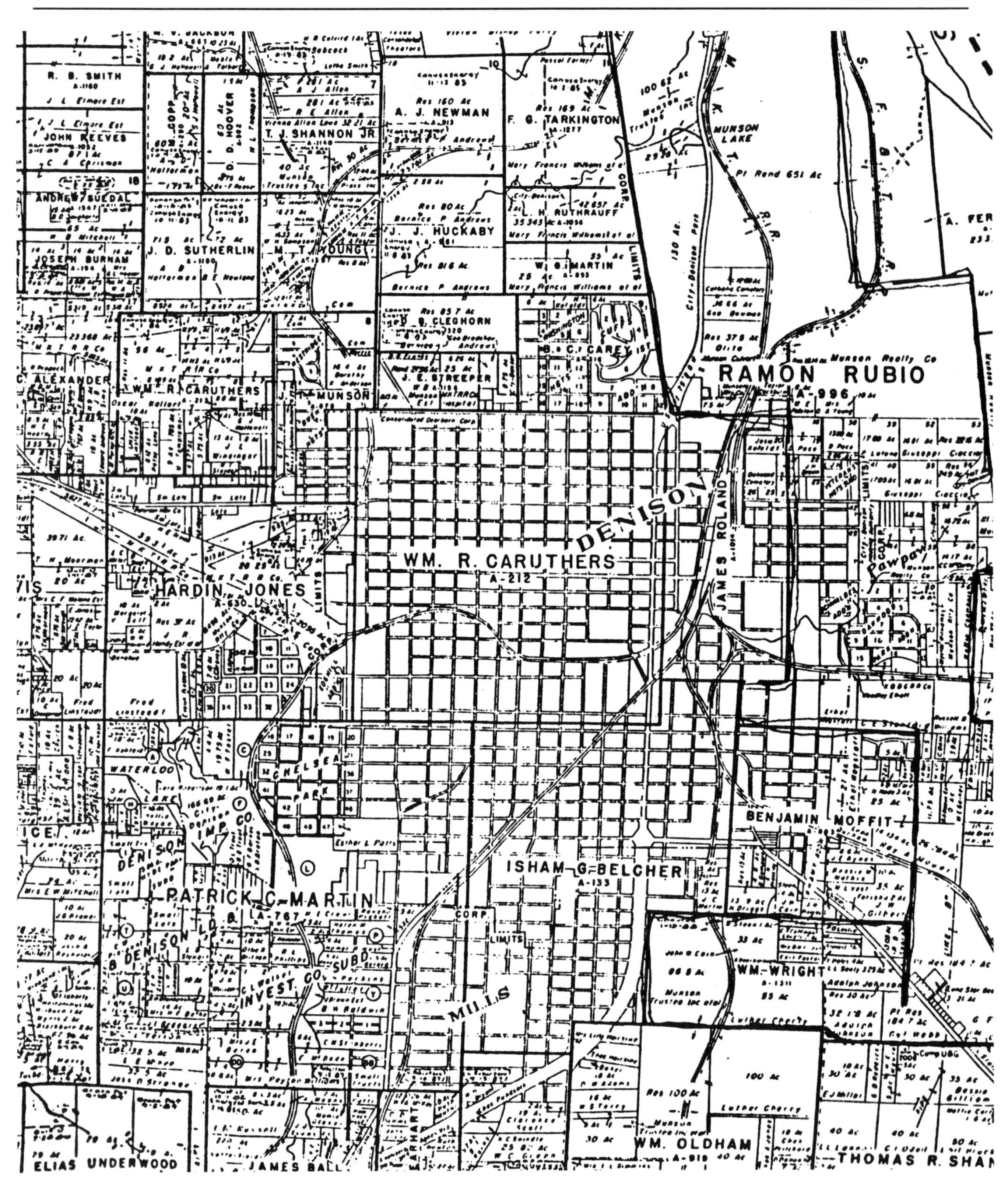

Abstract map showing plat of original town and its environs.
— Tone Abstract Company

first lots — at least fifty prospective buyers gathered on the townsite. In what is now the alley between the 200 blocks of Owings and Morgan streets, a motley array of tents, box houses and booths already had been set up. Businesses included a bakery, a clothing store, a drug store, and a tinshop. There was even a printing press, on which publisher George A. Cutler issued his *Red River City Journal* in red ink to signify the opposition of most of those on hand to naming the place "Denison."

Although Red River City was only a tent city peopled largely by prostitutes and gamblers, its name was coveted. Few people except Katy employees had ever heard of George Denison, but the name "Red River City" was known throughout the country. The hundreds of freighters who had reached Indian Territory via Colbert's Ferry and the drovers playing nursemaid to the herds that forded the river there had carried stories of the settlement to every railhead. Although the rival H&TC planned to build to the river site, residents of Katy's "baby" were confident that their town soon would become the gateway to Texas and that the original Red River City would disappear.

This confidence must surely have been boosted when the sale of lots began. The first bid was $100. From this it went up by fives and tens until S. A. Cook got the first lot for $250. It was at the northwest corner of Main and Austin. W. L. Hull bought the second, which was directly across Main, for $300. Some thought the prices were too high and left in disgust. However, by day's end, thirty-one lots had been sold for a total of $4,791 — an average of $154.54 each.

Katy's "baby" had entered the world a healthy infant, indeed. Its name, however, would remain "Denison."

Denison's first Union Station, built to accommodate Katy and H&TC trains. The McDougall Hotel was at the north end. The station served Denison's railroad needs until 1914, when the last Union Station was built.

Wagon and passengers crossing Red River on Colbert's Ferry.
— Ralph Douglas Collection

2

The Infancy

"The New Year, like an infant heir to the whole world, was waited for with welcomes, presents and rejoicing."

— Charles Dickens, "The Chimes" (1844)

With the initial sale of lots, Denison pioneers, like Dickens characters, felt that they were heirs to the whole world. They had to wait for their welcomes, presents and rejoicing, however, for two future events: the arrival of the first train and the formal incorporation of the town.

The completion of the railroad into Denison came three months and two days after the first lots were auctioned. It was a special Christmas gift of the Katy to its new "baby" and to all of Texas. The arrival of the first passenger train from the north was on Christmas Day, 1872.

This history-making arrival had been anticipated for days. When it happened, however, it was anticlimactic! Most of the cheering, drinking and joviality had come on Christmas Eve, when an unscheduled work train pulled into the Denison station unannounced.

It wasn't planned quite that way. The last rail from the Red River into Denison had been laid and the last spike driven on Saturday, December 21. Minor work remained to be completed on the new bridge across the river, however, and that was to be done on Monday, the twenty-third. This would give Katy General Manager Robert S. Stevens and Chief Engineer Otis B. Gunn time to get from their Sedalia, Missouri, headquarters to Colbert Station, the railroad's last stop in southern Oklahoma. Thus they could be aboard the work train that would test the rails and make the first entry into Denison.

By Tuesday afternoon, December 24, the weather was biting cold. The sky was overcast and snow flurries brought promise of the first "blue norther" of the year. Nevertheless, the construction train, piled high with rails and ties to test the strength of the new bridge and with 100 workers aboard, headed south out of Colbert Station. The private car of General Manager Stevens, crowded with railroad officials and important guests, was on the rear.

At Colbert's Ferry, Red River City rowdies lined the tracks to shout insults at the train. As the engineer took the hill from the river toward the new townsite, he tied down the whistle to alert the countryside that the first train ever to enter Texas from the north was on the way. By the time he pulled into the Denison station four miles away, practically everyone within earshot of the piercing whistle was on hand.

There was no formal greeting, nor organized program of any kind. The town had been taken by surprise, and the crowd reacted spontaneously with enthusiastic cheers, then headed toward the handful of saloons to celebrate the arrival of the first train and Christmas Eve.

The Historic Moment That Wasn't

Thus the arrival twenty-four hours later on Christmas afternoon of the first scheduled passenger train was not the celebrated event it was meant to be. Pat Tobin, a twenty-five-year-old engineer, was at the throttle of No. 15, the tiny, diamond-stacked, wood-burning locomotive. He wheezed his train of two coaches and a Pullman Palace car into the station at 7:00 P.M. A small crowd braved the cold, but there was little fanfare. Few even realized that among the 100 passengers were Santana and Big Tree, the famed Indian chiefs, who were being taken to state prison.

Santana was a Comanche chief. Although the

This was the first Katy depot in the new town of Denison.
— *From the collection of Robert C. Stevens, Pittsford, NY*

Comanches constantly had harassed Texas settlements, Santana had been considered something of a friend. He had represented his tribe on March 2, 1847, when he met on the banks of the San Saba River in the Hill Country to sign a peace treaty with John O. Muesebach, the founder of the town of Fredericksburg.

Not so with Big Tree. A Kiowa, he was noted for his raids on settlers. On May 17, 1871, with Santana and others, he had led an attack on a wagon train in Young County. They killed the wagonmaster and six teamsters, and scalped another, tied him to a wagon wheel and burned him. Others survived, but with injuries. The incident became known as the Salt Creek Massacre. Santana and Big Tree were arrested, brought to trial at Fort Sill in Indian Territory and sentenced to life in prison. Since their crimes were committed in Texas, they were sent to the state penitentiary in Huntsville. Denison was a stop on the way.

These famous criminals attracted little attention from the assembly at the Katy depot. The usually astute editor of the *Daily News,* B. C. Murray, who wrote only a three-paragraph story about the arrival of the train, did nothing more than mention the names of the Indians. He could not foresee that Santana and Big Tree would change the political history of Texas.

The Indians had been convicted of terrible depredations, but they had been given a fair trial. Even in 1873, however, dissidents were wont to show their displeasure at governmental actions with which they disagreed. Reservation Indians already had started a movement to free their colleagues.

Hoping to soothe them, President U.S. Grant later summoned all of the tribal leaders to Washington. The chiefs refused to pow-wow, however, unless their brother chieftains, Santana and Big Tree, also were invited. Grant asked Edmund J. Davis, the Republican governor who was a virtual dictator of Texas, to pardon them. Davis refused, but he did parole them under heavy guard long enough for them to board a Katy train for Washington and attend the White House meeting.

Judging from the reaction, Davis might as well have given them a full pardon. Texans were infuriated that the governor had released the Indians even temporarily. In the 1873 elections, voters overwhelmingly rejected Davis and elected his Democratic opponent, Richard Coke. This restored that political party to power in the state for more than a century.

Although the arrival of the first train and its notorious passengers made no headlines, it heralded the start of the real growth of Katy's "baby." Within a few years, Denison would become the busiest and most important transportation center in the state — the true "Gate City of Texas," a slogan which it still proudly proclaims.

It was a different situation sixty years later when Pat Tobin, still hale and hearty at eighty-five, rode the locomotive cab of the Katy's famed *Texas Special* into Denison from the north on Christmas morning, 1932. More than 500 turned out in the winter darkness to greet him. Among the old timers present were A. H. Coffin, who had laid out the town, and Dr. Alex W. Acheson, Denison's first physician.

New Town in Texas

If the residents of Katy's "baby" failed to celebrate adequately the arrival of their unusual Christmas gift, they made up for it when word came from Austin that the legislature had approved the incorporation of the City of Denison.

The formal certificate of its birth did not come until February 8, 1873, when Governor Edmund J.

"THE TOWN THAT KATY BUILT"
1872

Davis signed the act creating the new town. William H. Day, among the first to buy a lot, had been sent to the Capitol to lobby the necessary paperwork through. His telegram to B. C. Murray, publisher of the *Daily News,* announcing that Denison would become a legal entity on March 7, set off an impromptu and frenzied celebration and parade by the estimated 3,000 residents who already called the place home.

Murray's account of the revelry indicates that the population was surprisingly incongruous, if not motley, for a Texas frontier town. He described it this way:

"Almost every nation on earth was represented. There was the American, vastly in number, the Englishman, the Russian, the Frenchman, the German, the Turk and even decadent China was severally represented. They fell into one another's arms and caressed with joy."

Harrison Tone prepared the abstracts on the sale of lots in the new townsite and became Denison's first historian.

— *Denison Herald*

The merriment that lasted far into the night was a needed safety valve for the hearty souls who had elected to build a new town on the rolling plains of the Red River Valley. Except for drinking, gambling, fighting and patronizing prostitutes, there was little recreation. Even day to day living was primitive in the extreme.

Numbers of homes had been built of rough, unpainted pine. Most had no water except from communal wells. Nine small, crude hotels were operating and were fully booked by the more affluent settlers who could afford the $1-a-day charge for a bed and meals. However, according to Harrison Tone, a charter citizen and the town's first historian, most of the residents were still living in tents or their wagons a year after the first lots were sold. Some slept on the ground.

In an article he wrote for the *Daily News* on September 23, 1873, the town's first birthday, Tone said:

> (The residents') morning toilet consisted of a wash, frequently a dry one, and a running of the fingers through the hair, and their "house" was set in order by rolling up the blanket on which they had slept. If, as was often the case, they had no blanket, they had to rise from the ground and shake themselves when they were ready for the business of the day.
>
> Meals were taken at restaurants (there were five); when one person had no sooner risen from the bench, another took his place, the plate was hastily wiped upon a dirty towel and the meal went on as before.
>
> The same bill of fare was served up with unvarying regularity, morning, noon and night. It consisted of bread without butter, coffee without milk and beef steak which had to be fished out of the vat in which it was swimming.

Tone wrote that despite the hardships, "the greatest good feeling prevailed . . . and all grew hearty and jovial while roughing it."

Prosperity, more than anything else, inspired these early settlers to endure. During the first few months, $90,000 worth of building lots were sold. Lumber demand was so great that the railroads and

This cabin is believed to be the first residence built in the new townsite. It was built by Dr. Alexander Morrison in the 800 block of West Main on the approximate site of today's Waples Memorial Methodist Church.
— *H. D. Morgan drawing*

mills hundreds of miles away saw profits soar. Harrison Tone wrote that customers besieged nearby mills day and night, sometimes fighting over each individual board as it fell from the saw.

How did Denison appear to an outsider? When the town was only four months old, Edward King, a writer for *Scribner's Magazine*, rode the Katy down from St. Louis and spent several days there. The article he wrote for the July 1873 issue of that famous magazine presented one visitor's unbiased view of the place:

"All around us was Babel — a wild rush of business, a glory in affairs, an unbounded delight in mere labor, which at once oppressed and appalled us," he began his article. "The slightest indication of progress was pointed out as a gigantic prospect for the future solidity of Denison. Indeed, all of these enthusiastic pioneers of a new civilization were justified in their seemingly wild prophecies of greatness."

Everywhere King saw the spirit that would make Denison what its founders dreamed it could be.

"The earnestness of the new town, the almost religious quality of its ambition, was amusing as well as inspiring," he wrote. "All of the inhabitants were determined to make out of this irregular group of one-story wooden buildings, sitting confusedly on the high rolling land four miles south of the Red River, one of the principal capitals of the universe. Their zeal was as reviving as new wine."

He was surprised at the cosmopolitan population.

"(It) is not safe in a new town like Denison to judge a man . . . by his outer garb and manners," he said. "The huge hulking fellow with one cheek distended with tobacco, and with his clothes all so disposed that they seem to have been thrown upon him, will answer you with all the courtesy and grace of a high-bred gentleman. The roughness is of the exterior only."

And so the progress continued. Slowly more and more houses supplanted the tents and wagons. Chairs began to replace wooden boxes as furniture. Some of the better hotels provided mattresses, sheets and even pillows for their beds. Paths became streets, and Denison began developing into a city.

Who's on First?

Most of the new growth came from the immigrants from all over who streamed in behind the railroad. Also, residents of Katy's baby soon had infants of their own. But for more than a century, there has been a controversy as to who was the first child born in the new town.

Denison Nelson, who ran a meat market for years at 931 West Main, always claimed the honor. He boasted that he was given the name "Denison" by his parents in recognition of the fact that the

This drawing was made of a Katy passenger train of the 1870s.
— *Katy Railroad Archives*

stork arrived at the Nelson place within a few days after the first lots were sold.

If so, the *Denison Daily News* wasn't notified. It reported that "the first boy to open his eyes in Denison was Sam Hanna, Jr., son of our esteemed fellow citizen, Sam Hanna, Sr., born December 1, 1872."

Also, there are two versions as to who was the first baby girl. On May 5, 1873, the *Daily News* announced the arrival of Texana Denison McElvaney. This news was so exciting that James P. Dumas, who developed an addition to the town, presented lot No. 5, block No. 8, to her family as a gift. The address was 318 East Shepherd. However, there is no record of the John G. McElvany family except the mention in the deed to the property. It is possible that the gift deed was never exercised.

In the 1930's, another claimant for the honor came forward. Mrs. W. C. Schwendiman, then living in Oakland, California, and aged ninety, sent a letter to the Denison *Herald* and enclosed a photograph of her late daughter, Dora. Mrs. Schwendiman wrote that their family had arrived in Denison before the first lots were sold. They built a home at 202 West Owings, and Mr. Schwendiman opened a store in the 100 block of West Main.

Dora, one of seven Schwendiman children, was born March 19, 1873. Her mother wrote "that she was the first Denison-born girl to graduate from the new school." Dora later attended Harshaw's Business College and married Herbert L. McLow. She died in 1902.

Who actually were the first infants born in Katy's town may never be settled.

Uncle Sam's Mail

If the proud parents of these infants sent birth notices to distant friends, there was no problem. The Denison area had mail service before the townsite existed.

The Butterfield Overland Mail had started operations between St. Louis and San Francisco in 1858, entering Texas via Colbert's Ferry and using Sand Springs, on the southwestern edge of what now is Denison, as a rest and water stop. In 1867, Ben Ficklin started another mail and passenger route from Fort Smith, Arkansas, into Texas and also stopped at Sand Springs en route to an already bustling place called Sherman.

The platting of the Denison townsite and the arrival of the first train on Christmas, 1872, did not immediately bring a U.S. post office. Mail was dropped off and picked up at the office of the Denison Town Company near the present Forrest Park. By 1873, however, a post office was in operation. The exact location isn't clear, but contemporary newspapers placed it on Skiddy (now Chestnut) Street in either the 100 or 200 block. It was open every day of the week, including Sunday.

Little is known of the first postmaster, a Mr. Nelson, but his deputy was Harrison Tone. He liked being deputy so much that he spent between $500 and $600 of his own money to make the post office building more presentable.

For several years the location of the post office changed almost as often as did the postmasters. From Skiddy Street it moved to the corner of Main and Burnett, the later site of the now demolished Security Building. It then was moved to the center of the 200 block of West Main, next to Main and Rusk (where Team Bank stands in 1991), then back to the southwestern corner of Main and Burnett. Eventually it was located at the corner of Woodard and Rusk, site of the present Munson Building. Its final move was to its present location, where the current building was erected in 1911.

Farmers Had to Wait

Until 1888, there was no mail delivery to homes or offices. That year, free delivery was started and has continued. However, there is one innovation introduced in Texas by the Denison post office that has to be stated carefully to be accurate.

Many stories have appeared claiming that Denison pioneered the free delivery of rural mail in 1901 — and this is true. However, it should be made clear that this only inaugurated the free delivery of such mail. On August 1, 1889, the La Grange post office started delivering mail to Fayette County farmers, but a fee was charged for this extra service.

During years when the railroads were the principal transport for intercity mail, Denison bragged that its postal service was among the nation's fastest and best. A first-class letter (postage three cents) mailed before 5:00 P.M. was assured delivery in St. Louis or Houston the next morning. For an additional ten-cent "special delivery" stamp, a courier would personally take it to the address. In those days, the postman always rang twice — he came each morning and again in the afternoon.

Then postal authorities in Washington decided to "improve" the operation. In 1952, transporting the mail began to be shifted from the railroads to trucks and airlines. The decision was a severe blow to Denison, both to its economy and its excellent mail service.

Of the forty-three passenger trains that served the city each twenty-four hours, thirty-three were designated as mail transports. As a result, Denison was the district headquarters of the Railway Mail Service, which employed 111 persons. Included were 104 railway postal clerks who rode the trains and sorted and distributed the mail en route. The speed and quality of the service was far superior to that of any nation in the world.

It was profitable, too. In 1952, when 93% of all mail was moved by train, the operation netted the post office a profit of $21,918,000. That same year, the 7% of the mail that was sent by other transport created a loss of $21,916,000 and a slowdown in delivery. Nevertheless the transfer of mail transport from rail to air and highways continued, and this became a major factor in the demise of Denison's railroads.

Instead of forty-three passenger trains through Denison, now there are none. When the Railway Mail Service ended, fifty-four families lost their livelihood. The cost to mail a first-class letter has skyrocketed over the years from three cents to twenty-nine cents (1991 price) — almost 300%. Parcel post has all but disappeared. Yet the U.S. Post Office itself has continued to run up increasing deficits each year.

The loss of the Railway Mail Service and the railroad trains that made it possible was an economic blow from which these transportation giants and the City have never recovered.

3

Discipline for Katy's Baby

"As new conditions and problems arise beyond the power of men and women to meet as individuals, it becomes the duty of Government itself to find new remedies."

—Franklin Delano Roosevelt

The celebration on February 8, 1873, of the formal recognition by the legislature and governor that Denison was a legal city lasted most of the night. It was not until the next morning that the celebrants, many still in an alcoholic haze, faced the reality of what this new status meant to them as full-fledged Denisonians.

Suddenly they realized that Katy's baby, like all infants, demanded immediate and thoughtful care. It was something that few had considered when the town was going through its birth pangs. Now it was a responsibility they didn't want to assume.

For starters, theirs was a town without funds and without established taxable values. It was without water, without fire and police protection, without a government — indeed, it lacked everything necessary to make a municipality a home. Suddenly the "Infant Wonder" had become a Frankenstein! The question was: Who could control the monster?

No one had the right to vote because the city was only one day old officially and no voting rights had been established. Furthermore, there was no one for whom to vote. What sane person would stand for public office when it appeared that there was much to do and no funds with which to do it?

In the bill chartering the City of Denison, the legislature had included one bit of fiscal hope. The lawmakers authorized the new town to issue scrip to meet its obligations until it could form a government and start levying taxes. That would at least provide funds for basic operations. Also, the citizenry was given the right to name a provisional mayor and council until such time as proper elections could be held.

Fortunately Denison had among its diverse population an individual superbly equipped to become its leader. He was L. S. Owings.

Owings was hardly the kind of settler one expected to find in an infant town still wrapped in the swaddling clothes of a railroad. A native of Tennes-

L. S. Owings, who was the governor of Arizona Territory before he became the first mayor of Katy's new town in Texas.

— *Chamber of Commerce Collection*

see, a physician who didn't practice medicine, and something of an adventurer, he had come to Texas in 1850. He became involved in real estate, promoting new towns along stage routes. He was the co-founder of Helena, the Karnes County town he named for his wife.

The Governor Who Became a Mayor

He was, in fact, one of the organizers of that county and had served in the Sixth Texas Legislature as its representative. In 1859, when money became tight in Texas and slavery a controversial issue, he moved to New Mexico. There he led the establishment of an illegal government in an effort to force Congress to grant territorial status to southern New Mexico. The dissidents met in April 1860 at Tucson, in the name of the Territory of Arizona, and adopted a provisional constitution. Owings was elected the first governor.

His friend and personal secretary was Bredette C. Murray, who doubled as editor of the Mesilla, New Mexico *Times*. In August 1861, when Governor Owings' government was replaced by the military, he and Murray both left New Mexico and returned to Texas. In 1872, they moved to Denison to await the arrival of the Katy, and Owings started a livery stable. Murray founded the Denison *Daily News*.

The *Sunday Gazetteer*, like the *Daily News*, was important to early Denison. Each was founded by B. C. Murray, who was both publisher and editor.

— *Chamber of Commerce Collection*

Thus it was that Denison chose as its first mayor a former governor of a U.S. territory — a distinction no other frontier town can claim. His fellow citizens, urged by Murray's support in his newspaper, apparently agreed that nobody was more qualified to handle the affairs of the new town.

The town charter called for the election of a mayor and three aldermen. J. M. Stratton, a dealer in hides, whiskey and wool, was selected, along with N. C. Taylor, real estate broker, merchant and money-lender. The third was Murray, the outspoken publisher of the *Daily News*. The council met for the first time on March 13, 1873.

The first meeting was perfunctory since no ordinances had been drawn as yet empowering them to govern. They did name Charles Maurice, a real estate dealer, as city recorder; appointed Dr. Julian C. Feild, another early medical doctor, as city physician, and made J. C. McDowell city marshal and chief of police. McDowell was given a deputy and four officers to keep the peace. J. G. McElvaney was appointed city attorney. The council also named a citizens' committee to draw up ordinances.

Uniforms on Lay-Away?

The marshal and police were told to buy uniforms of "a blue blouse coat with brass buttons, blue pants and a Panama hat for summer wear" and a blue cap to replace the hat in winter. Since the town had no funds, the officers were required to buy their own outfits, paying for them over three months.

Another concern, as it was in every frontier town with wooden buildings and no running water,

Time marches on, and motorized vehicles slowly replaced horse-drawn wagons in fire-fighting equipment.
— *Denison Fire Department Archives*

"Good Bye."

WE'RE GOING TO KANSAS AND TEXAS.

This early Katy ad helped draw settlers to the new towns along its route.

— *Katy Railroad Archives*

was fire. There was no thought of establishing a department of paid firemen — the budget wouldn't allow it. However, a volunteer fire department was formed, a single horse-drawn fire cart was purchased and a warning bell installed on Main Street. When the bell sounded, the volunteers rushed to a central point, got the cart and did their best to control the blaze.

One of the first acts of the aldermen was to start the process of taxation. The first tax was levied only three weeks after the first council was seated! On April 11, 1873, the citizens were ordered to pay three-fourths of 1% of the total value of their property as an ad valorem tax. However, the new property tax, another levy on occupations, fines paid in court and dog license fees were not enough to meet expenses. The young town was soon in financial difficulty.

Despite budget problems, the city fathers took time to do two things which they felt were necessary for posterity. First, an official seal was ordered from St. Louis. Engraved by one W. C. Bernard, who specialized in producing such accessories, the seal was a work of art. It had a steer's head in the center, surrounded by the words "The City of Denison, Texas."

A Grand Flag for a Grand Town

Although minutes of early meetings of the aldermen don't mention it, it seems that they also decided that their town needed a flag. They adopted one, then promptly forgot about it. Then in 1936, when I was writing my first book, *A Short History of Denison, Texas*, A. H. Coffin, who had been at the first council meeting, mentioned the flag. He didn't think one had ever been made up, but he recalled some of the design.

Ten years later, when I was digging through some research files in the Fort Worth Public Library, I found a document stating that Denison had, indeed, designed a city flag. It consisted of two blocks of green on top, representing the green grass of the Indian Territory, and two white blocks below, symbolic of the cotton fields of Texas. They were bisected by a vertical black stripe to indicate how the Katy Railroad connected the two, and were separated horizontally by a band of red for the Red River. In the center was a gold star representing Denison, described in the document as "a jewel at the crossroads of a great river and at the interweaving of two great sections of the country."

I sent the information to Claud Easterly of the Denison *Herald*. What Easterly did with it, I don't know. I never heard from him. But in 1968, I told the story of the flag in a monthly column I wrote for the old *Texas Parade* Magazine. Suddenly I began getting letters from Denison, including one from City Manager E. N. Delashmutt. It seemed that the then mayor, Joseph W. Gay, and the city council thought the time had come to make the flag official.

On November 13, 1968, the council met and approved Resolution 707 adopting the 1873 banner. Using a sketch that I furnished them, the Denison Girls Club took the role of Betsy Ross for the community and made the first flag.

Although my painstaking research was not mentioned in the document signed by Mayor Gay and City Clerk Louise Blanton, they sent me an official copy. On the affixed city seal, however, a lone star had replaced the Longhorn steer that graced the first one.

At any rate, the green and white flag of Denison not only flies proudly over City Hall now, but an ornate metal version is affixed to the front of the building for all to see.

However, in 1873, neither the flag nor the official seal helped the town's budget problems. By June of that year, the city was more than $2,000 in the red.

For a while it seemed that the prediction of Sherman newspapers that Denison would end in bankruptcy had some validity.

It's the Woman Who Pays

The problem was solved in part by collecting fees from the population of prostitutes and those who operated the bawdy houses. Brothel keepers had to ante up a $5 fee each week to the city, and each of their inmates was assessed $1. These funds were distributed equally between the members of the local police force.

This not only pleased the marshals, but it eradicated most of the bribes that this segment of the business community had been paying for police "protection."

However, the ladies of the evening and their

landlords didn't object to the new fees as much as they did to another fiat by the lawmakers. They were ordered to move their establishments off of Main Street.

Most of the brothels and saloons moved one block south to Skiddy (now Chestnut Street). Francis Skiddy was one of the directors of the Katy and a prominent businessman, but his name seemed to lend itself to such an entertainment area.

Much of the political action during Denison's first year involved leadership other than that of Mayor Owings. In ill health when he took the job in March, he served only until his resignation in May. Although his tenure was short, Owings left a lasting legacy. He founded the educational system and led the effort that resulted in the building of the first free graded public school in Texas.

He also left a fiscal problem.

When Owings resigned, J. M. Stratton was named mayor pro tem. The town's treasury already was in the red, but this did not discourage candidates for the office. There was a spirited race to be the first elected chief executive. The honor went to Frank Schrader with 106 votes. He defeated S. A. Cook, purchaser of the first lot in town, who received 88 votes.

There weren't many qualified voters. Out of a population of 3,917, only 627 were of voting age. Of these, 250 registered and 194 actually cast ballots. One possible reason for the lack of interest may have been the flagrant irregularities in the balloting.

How to Get Elected Without Trying

In that first official election, for example, a candidate for alderman from the Third Ward was Dr. H. Mozeley. The polling place for that ward was Dr. H. Mozeley's Drug Store. The judge appointed to watch over the election was Dr. H. Mozeley. It's hardly surprising that the winner in that ward was the same Dr. Mozeley.

By whatever means or margin the mayoralty may have been won, few of those elected served their full terms. By November 27, Schrader had given up trying to govern and quit. His replacement as acting mayor? Dr. H. Mozeley, of course.

The good doctor ordered an immediate election. This time Ed Perry got the job — the fifth mayor of one kind or another in the first year of the town's history.

Despite the mayors' game of musical chairs, Denison's fiscal problem worsened. It was only heightened in July 1873, when the citizenry voted to issue $10,000 in bonds to attract one of its first industries — a plant to slaughter and ship up to 700 beeves daily in new refrigerator cars. The same month saw the council vote an $800 annual salary for the mayor and authorize $875 in attorney fees to fight an injunction brought by some disgruntled citizens to prevent the elected councilmen from taking office.

The officials also decided they needed a regular place to meet and rented fancy quarters on Main Street known as the "Gold Rooms" for $45 a month.

While these expenditures added to the budget crisis, it was one of the town's proudest achievements that brought its government to the verge of bankruptcy. Under the leadership of Mayor Owings and the first Board of Aldermen, Denison spent more than $45,000 to erect the first free graded public school in Texas. However, by September 1, 1873, with the new school under construction, the town fathers had to face the fact that the treasury was empty.

In an unusual action for a political body, they began retrenching by cutting official salaries. Everybody from the mayor down received pay cuts that saved the taxpayers several hundred dollars. The city surveyor was removed entirely from the payroll and told that he would have to subsist on fees for his services. Even the police force was reduced from four officers to three. The city hospital was closed and the property ordered sold.

To find more money, they started assessing residents for work on the streets unless the property owner chose to help with the grading and improvement himself. A $2 annual fee was voted on those owning dogs. Barbers somehow had been overlooked when the first council levied a tax on occupations, so a $100 levy was placed on them.

By adding a tax here and increasing a fine there, the town managed to muddle through its financial crisis and make some physical improvements, too. It authorized an effort to get stumps out of Gandy Street and required the building of sidewalks where deemed necessary — the cost to be paid by the property owners.

Denison continued its aldermanic form of government until March 21, 1907. Then it got a new charter and cut its governing body from a mayor and one alderman from each ward to two city commissioners and a mayor, all elected at large. In 1913, the city adopted home rule. The present charter providing for a council-manager form of government was adopted in 1956.

Cool Water for Thirsty Souls

Such changes in the form of the municipal government often are necessary because of growth and altered conditions. However, they don't solve the everyday problems of running a town. Providing essential services like water, heat and light to a growing community is a continuing concern. It certainly was in 1872 and 1873.

The water supply was a major issue. However, Denison was fortunate in having as one of its first settlers a farmer who became an early utility "magnate."

He was J. K. Miller, who had settled near the Denison townsite twelve years before the Katy Railroad arrived. He had the foresight to build his home, located at what now is 1401 W. Walker, close to a spring flowing an abundance of clear, cold water. As other settlers moved in, he sold them enough water to satisfy their basic needs.

Miller's spring was a great asset, since many of the early residents could not afford to drill their own wells. However, the first city council recognized their needs and had a public well dug in the center of the intersection of Main Street and Austin Avenue. It was thirty-six-feet-deep and contained up to eight feet of water.

As quickly as possible, efforts were made to assure a larger, more permanent water supply. If a bulletin issued by the Denison Board of Trade in 1887 can be believed, a waterworks system was in place by the mid-1870's.

The publication, distributed at the State Fair of Texas in an attempt to attract new business to the growing railroad center, stated that the system consisted of a standpipe 15 feet in diameter and 125 feet high. There were wells at fourteen locations connected by more than a mile of underground tunnels. The wells produced up to a million gallons of water daily.

For reasons unknown, the 1887 brochure doesn't mention that Denison's dependence on the wells was about to end. In 1886, a private company had built the Waterloo pump station. The dam was completed the next year and the first sewer system installed. By 1909, the town also had completed Randell Lake. These two reservoirs supplied water needs until the completion of Denison Dam and the creation of Lake Texoma.

How to Turn Paraffin into Heat

Although water was plentiful, light and heat were not. Kerosene lamps and candles were the only source of light. Residents did their cooking on wood and coal stoves and heated their homes and businesses the same way. Wood was abundant locally and coal was easily available from the mines at McAlester, Oklahoma, a short haul on the Katy.

But better lighting was on the way and gas was the source. On March 1, 1876, the Denison Gas Works went into operation. The plant was on Mirick Avenue just south of Morgan Street. The manufactured gas was stored in a large, cylindrical tank supported by a cradle system that rose and fell as the production and use of gas varied.

At the time, most artificial gas was made from coal. The local operation, however, chose to use paraffin, a distillate made from gas, wood and petroleum. It proved to be less expensive than other artificial gas, which caused local newspapers to brag:

"The city is lighted at an expense of $3 per month per lamp post, while no other city in the State pays less than $5."

The newspaper ignored that another reason for the cheaper bills was the penury of the town council. That body ruled that lights were turned on only when there was no moon!

Originally gas was available to homes for both light and cooking, but to businesses only for lighting. Coal and wood stoves and fireplaces were the only heating units available until 1912, when natural gas came to Denison.

On November 15, 1889, electricity was introduced when the Denison Power & Light Co. was chartered. The incorporators were W. B. Munson, Sr., J. B. McDougall and John Scullin, who had supervised the laying of the Katy's rails into the new town. The initial generating system consisted of two 150-KVA. The motors were housed in a plant on South Mirick Avenue, where in 1991 the TU Electric still maintains a shop.

Lights Go On Part-time

Most electric utilities in that period did not provide twenty-four-hour service. The record doesn't indicate how much daily service was available in Denison. Based on the records in other communities at that time, however, it is likely that the generators operated only from dusk to midnight and from 5:00 A.M. to daylight. A few operated on designated afternoons when housewives were ironing, and some provided extra power on cloudy days. Since very few smaller communities in 1889 had round-the-clock electric service, it is likely that it also was limited in Denison.

In 1913, Munson and the others sold their interests in the electric utility to the recently organized Texas Power & Light Co. The new corporation was started to provide lines to transmit electricity to several North and East Texas towns. Almost immediately TP&L increased the generating capacity to 1,000 KVA.

This limited amount of available power continued until 1915, when the company brought its transmissions lines into the town, thus guaranteeing a steady supply of power. Denison was among the first towns in the area to receive this improved service. The demand was not great.

The average home had only six electrical drops, usually from the center of the ceiling of as many rooms. Each was fitted with a single bulb, usually bare. About the only use for electricity in the home was for lighting. Most of the electric appliances so common today — even irons — were not available. The heaviest single local demand for electricity was for a fifty-horsepower motor at the Denison Mill & Grain Co.

Electric power was costly. The luxury of well-lighted houses was limited to the more prosperous. The monthly charge was 15 cents per kilowatt for a minimum of 60 kilowatts, or $9 a month.

Number, Please?

With plenty of water and gas lights, Denison was regarded as a progressive town even before it got its first telephone in 1883.

Dr. Alexander Graham Bell had invented the instrument only seven years before and it was still regarded by many as a plaything. Denisonians always have been willing to try new ideas, however, and the first exchange boasted about fifty subscribers. The business expanded so rapidly that in 1886 a second telephone company was established. Denison remained a town with two competing phone companies until 1918.

This, of course, presented myriad problems. Businesses and homeowners who wanted to reach all other telephones had to install two separate lines and instruments. Even when the two companies merged, the difficulties remained. Each had used different equipment that was not compatible with the other. In 1923, however, Southwestern Bell took over the operations. For the first time, Denison had an integrated telephone system.

Inventions like the telephone, the electric light and stoves run by natural gas would have been called impossible dreams if they had been proposed as future possibilities to that first city council at its meeting on March 13, 1873. If, however, there was a philosopher among them, he would have responded with these words of Alcaeus written 600 years before Christ and quoted here at the beginning of Chapter 1:

> "What makes a city? Not houses finely rooted or the stones of walls well-builded, nay not canals or dockyards, but men able to use their opportunity."

Denison has been blest from the beginning with leadership able to use their opportunity.

4

Terminus of Ruffians

"When constabury duty's to be done,
The policeman's lot is not a happy one."
— William Schwenck Gilbert,
"The 'Bab' Ballads."

Katy intended its baby to be a principal terminal for the railroad — the temporary end of track for what the builders envisioned as one day being the greatest transportation gateway to the Southwest.

In 1872, however, the Indian Territory was the wildest of the Wild West — the haven of murderers, train robbers and outlaws of all kinds. Stealing horses and bootlegging whiskey into the Indian Territory (where alcohol was illegal) had become highly skilled professions. Denison, four miles as the crow flies from the sluggish river that separated Texas from the territory, became a kind of unofficial headquarters for a variety of criminals. It was a local brag that at least half of the almost 4,000 residents were "ruffians and the other offscourings of society."

Unlike most new towns in Texas, Denison was different from the start. It even looked different. Probably because of the state's Spanish-Mexican heritage, most new settlements sprang up around a central plaza or square with all manner of businesses intermingling around it.

Not Denison. It had no square. It was laid out as a perfect rectangle, using the points of the compass as pivots. Main Street, eighty feet wide, ran directly east and west. The avenues, less broad than Main, ran straight from north to south.

Denison was Zoned from the Start

Even if a square had been included in the town plat, the shops surrounding it would have been restricted. The Denison Town Company, in one of the earliest incidents of urban zoning in Texas history, limited tenants on the broad street only to those businesses that were deemed fit to occupy such a prominent address.

Saloons — of the quality of the Crystal Palace — were welcome so long as they kept the peace. An occasional pool hall was allowed, but most (plus gambling houses and dance halls that provided "hostesses" in the upstairs rooms) had to find space on Skiddy or other streets and avenues.

This early effort at zoning somehow separated, for the most part, the respectable citizens from the less desirable. It impressed a New York visitor who wrote:

> It was exceedingly remarkable that in a community (of ruffians) where there was not yet even an organized government there was not more of terrorism . . . There is no more danger to the life or limb of the traveler than may be incurred on Broadway (in New York).

It was the unique foresight of founder Robert S. Stevens and his Town Company that assured the safety of both residents and visitors in this new settlement that already had the reputation of being the toughest on the northern Texas border. In writing the charter for Denison, the organizers included a provision (Section 55) which gave it the power:

> To license, tax and regulate billiard tables, pen alleys, ball alleys, disorderly houses, tippling shops, barrooms, dramshops, other places where liquors are sold or dispensed, bawdy houses, houses of prostituion or assignation, gambling and gaming houses, lotteries, and all fraudulent devices and practices, and all kinds of indecencies . . .

Not only did this provision give the city government tight control over these operations, but it

This photo of Denison's present U.S. post office at the corner of Woodard Street and Rusk Avenue was made from the northeast corner of the site in October 1911, shortly after the building was completed. It has since been enlarged.

— *Photo courtesy of Postmaster James Hammons*

Drawing of the First Presbyterian Church. This denomination organized its church on December 23, 1872 — two days before the arrival of the first train.

— Ralph Douglas Collection

made sure that those who sinned would have to pay through taxes and/or fines for their indiscretions.

Despite the careful planning of the Town Company, however, it was both the best and worst of times for Denison. True it had a church (First Presbyterian) organized even before the first lots were sold. By the end of its first year, dozens of permanent homes had been built, a school established, a post office was in operation and even a hotel ("deluxe" by frontier standards) had been opened.

These economic and cultural advances, however, did not obliterate the shadow cast over the place by Skiddy (now Chestnut) Street just one block south of Main. As noted earlier, the street had been named to honor Francis Skiddy, an officer of the Katy Railroad. But to most residents, "Skiddy" denoted a place commonly called "rat alley."

In his book, *The Katy and the Great Southwest*, Masterson describes it this way:

> . . . The modern Skid Row couldn't compare with it. It was nothing but a ravine with the underbrush cleared away, and lined on both sides with the most depraved collection of tents, shacks and cotton cloth and board houses . . . Here, crowding each other into the befouled former watercourse, were the tented gambling hells, the hurdy-gurdy joints, lowest class saloons, cockfighting pits, variety houses, and the deadly "dovecoats" that served as houses of prostitution for all races, colors and creeds.

However, even Skiddy Street boasted a legitimate business or two. A grocery, a milliner and a print shop were tucked among what the preachers called "dens of iniquity."

Gun Control in 1873?

Apparently the operation of these establishments was not hampered by the frequent fights inspired by the neighboring gaming tables. Most arguments were settled by fists, and shootings were rare. Even then, Texas had stringent laws about packing arms. There were gun-fights on Skiddy (and sometimes on Main), but not as often as some of the stories related by old-timers would indicate. At least, they went unreported in the files of the *Daily News*, the only record still extant.

While Denison's resident population included a large number of unwelcome citizens, most of the ruffians called the Indian Territory home. They came to Denison to drink, carouse and buy whiskey to bootleg to the Indians. Few stayed on their good behavior when in Katy's town.

Contributing to Denison's unsavory reputation were characters known only as Rowdy Joe, Monte Jack, Cherokee Joe and others who had frequent run-ins with the town's three-man police squad. Ladies of the evening such as Liz, "Dirty Legs" Kitty and others of their ilk did little to improve the quality of the citizenry.

Although J. C. McDowell, who had the dual title of police chief and city marshal, and his little force did a good job of keeping the peace, more help was on the way. With Denison finally chartered and a local government in place, Grayson County commissioners decided it was time to recognize the town's existence. They promoted Sherman's city marshal, Lee (Red) Hall, to deputy sheriff and sent him to help clean up the crime-ridden town.

Hall, a schoolteacher turned cop, not only succeeded but became a kind of regional legend in the mold of the fictional Marshal Dillon of Abilene, Kansas.

Born Leigh Hall in Lexington, North Carolina, the staunch Presbyterian son of a surgeon came to Texas when he was twenty. He taught school in

In the 1920s, automobiles had replaced horses and buggies, and Main Street was no longer the terminus of ruffians.
— *Denison Herald*

VIEW OF MAIN STREET, DENISON TEXAS. 1878
PHOTOGRAPHED, BY GEORGE PERKINS.

Six years after the first lots were sold, Main Street was still building.
— *Collection of Donna Hunt*

By Christmas Day, 1872, when the first train arrived, Denison had taken on some semblance of a permanent settlement.
— *Katy Railroad Archives*

Grayson County for two years. In 1871, he became city marshal of Sherman and changed the spelling of his first name to "Lee" because it looked more masculine. An intelligent, shrewd and sociable man, he had a reputation for courage and unflinching nerve. He was told he would need it when he took over in Denison, "where lawless men are as thick as fiddlers in hell."

Hall already knew that "the policeman's lot is not a happy one," but he seemed to bear a charmed life. It was said that at least 100 men wanted to kill him, and he was ambushed, shot at and beaten many times. He always survived. He captured many of the outlaws that used Denison as their base for forays into the territory and killed at least one. Although he served less than two years (in 1873 and 1874) as deputy sheriff, the town's reputation for law and order had shown great improvement. Hall went on to become a Texas Ranger, Indian agent and an army officer in the Spanish-American War. He died in 1911.

Deputy Sheriff Red Hall was the soft-spoken deputy sheriff who helped bring law and order to the "terminus of ruffians."

— *Drawing from Scribner's Magazine*

When the Bride Said "No"

Although Deputy Hall and the Denison city marshals did the best they could to keep the behavior of the populace under control, Denison was destined to remain a wide open town for decades. Even the new bride of W. B. Munson refused to live in his adopted town. He brought her to Denison following their marriage in Dallas. After a short time, she decided that the place was too rowdy and insisted that they move to Sherman. It was several years before she agreed that it was safe to return to the town her husband had helped found.

Unfortunately, the Munsons had returned to Denison before the arrival of Dick Glass, the most notorious desperado to inhabit these parts. Glass, a black man, used Denison as a supply depot for the whiskey he shipped into Oklahoma Territory aboard Colbert's Ferry. Any kind of liquor was taboo anywhere in the territory, and the Indians would pay almost any price to get it. When Glass was not sneaking this profitable cargo across the river, he headed a gang of mixed bloods (Indian and black) that plundered and murdered throughout the southern boundary lands of the territory.

It was whiskey purchased from Denison saloons that finally ended Glass' life. In June 1885, he and a band of blacks were en route to the Seminole Indian nation with a wagon load of firewater. Officers stopped them at a point thirty miles west of Colbert. When Glass fired on them, they killed him.

Four years later, in 1889, what had been Indian Territory was opened to settlement. Whiskey-running from Denison no longer was lucrative and those involved in the business slowly disappeared from the scene. This did not change Denison's reputation for rowdiness for many more years, however.

Sherman citizens were delighted. Denisonians early on had dubbed that county seat "the Holy City." In comparison to Katy's town, the term was an apt description of Sherman. Although both towns had saloons and brothels, Denison had many more. By the 1940's, sin had disappeared or at least gone underground in Sherman, but bootlegging illegal whiskey continued to thrive in Denison, as did prostitution. Until the beginning of World War II, a favorite pastime for Shermanites and other visitors was to drive down the 100 block of West Main Street and point out the small hotels directly across from City Hall that doubled as brothels.

5

Git Along Little Dogie

"There's a long, long trail a-winding
Into the land of my dreams . . ."
— Stoddard King, "The Long, Long Trail" (1913)

The famous Chisholm Trail, like the Katy Railroad, can trace its roots to Denison.

In fact, so can the business of ranching in Texas as we know it today. Except for the genius of an Illinois entrepreneur who adopted Denison as his home, there might never have been a Chisholm Trail. And without that most famous of all the routes to markets, cattle raising in Texas in the 1870's would have been devastated.

When the Civil War ended, Texas was destitute. Soldiers coming home from the war found that their cattle had run wild and multiplied by the millions. Like those returning from wars throughout history, they faced the question of how to pick up their lives and feed their families.

The answer was on their long untended farms and ranches, now overrun with cattle. Those in the North and East wanted beef. They were willing and able to pay good prices for it. The problem was how to get the cattle to market on the hoof. Railroads still were largely non-existent in Texas, and trailing stock north over mostly unmapped trails was a gamble. Some who tried it lost fifty percent of their herds along the way.

Two events happened that would change this picture and make ranching an economic success. One was the birth of a new kind of job — the full-time cowboy. The other was the foresight of Joseph G. McCoy. He planned the route and arranged for the mapping of the best and most famous trail ever devised to get cattle to a railhead and then to market.

It's true that the Chisholm, this largest of all of the Southwestern cattle trails, already existed when the area on which Denison sits was still prairie. But it was McCoy, a man who later would choose Denison as his home, who conceived the idea for the trail and for whom many believe it should have been named.

Of Cattle Trails and Railroads

McCoy, a cattle trader, saw a way to make the Kansas Pacific Railroad (and himself) richer and also save the cattle industry in Texas. He knew that the country east of the Mississippi River and north of the Mason-Dixon Line was hungry for beef. He knew that a Longhorn steer, worth maybe $6 in Texas, would bring four times as much anywhere east of Kansas City. The KP Railroad could get them to market quickly and inexpensively if ranchers in Texas could drive the cattle to a railhead.

It was not a new idea. The first cattle drive in Texas was in the 1500's, when padres at the Spanish missions drove herds to market in New Orleans. Over the years a network of such trails had sprung up all over the state south of Waco. In a single year, 1866, an estimated 250,000 head had pushed up trails to Missouri and Kansas markets.

One — the Shawnee Trail — had started before the Civil War. It began on the Brazos River at Waco, continued along the present route of Interstate 35 to Dallas, then along what is now U.S. 75 to where Denison now stands. From this point, drovers had a choice of crossing the Red River at Colbert's Ferry or Preston. The trail continued across Indian Territory and stopped at the railhead in Sedalia, Missouri.

In the 1860's, trailing cattle up from South Texas and through the Indian Territory was no problem. But after the war, some points along the older trails in Kansas and Missouri started charging tolls on the herds. Also, quarantines prohibited

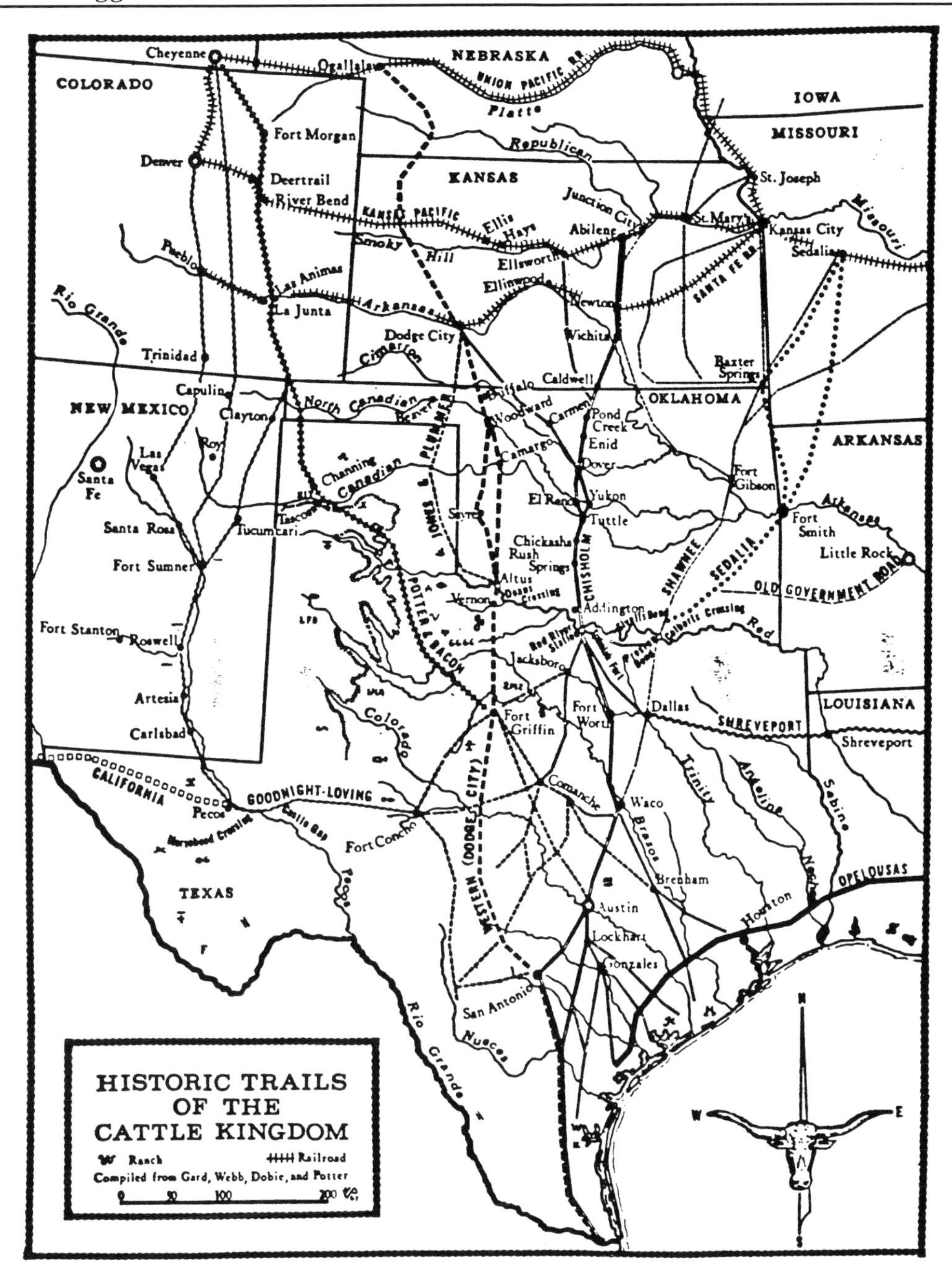

the cattle from entering certain areas, forcing drovers to detour their stock along unknown and unmarked routes. Farms, too, had sprung up on the open range and many farmers didn't hesitate to use guns to keep the moving cattle off their lands.

McCoy was confident that he could solve the problem. He believed that if a route could be developed that avoided these barriers and bypassed communities and towns, hundreds of herds would converge at a convenient railhead. He proposed to the KP Railroad that it make Abilene, a dismal settlement in western Kansas, such a cattle shipping center. His trail would be the means to get them there.

The railroad bought his idea and Abilene became the most famous "cowtown" in American history. Hundreds of thousands of cattle were delivered there over the famous trail from Texas which McCoy had a hand in designing.

To many, it would always be known as the McCoy Trail rather than the Chisholm. It was he who had it mapped out in 1867. It began in Waco, went north through Fort Worth and crossed into the Indian Territory at Red River Station in Montague County. That it was named for Jesse Chisholm, a half-breed Indian guide, instead of McCoy, was something of a fluke.

Years before, Chisholm, who guided wagon trains from his home on the North Canadian River in Indian Territory to a trading post on the Arkansas River, followed a route he had carved out of the wilderness. It seems that the first drovers up the trail to Abilene in 1867 followed Chisholm's visible wagon ruts and began to refer to it as "Chisholm's Trail." The name stuck, and Joseph McCoy lost the opportunity to win recognition in the geography of the West.

Instead he earned for himself at least a footnote to history by moving to the Katy's new baby in Texas and attempting to make it as famous a cowtown as he had made Abilene, Kansas.

T. L. Rankin, a friend of McCoy, had been one of the early arrivals in Denison. The town was less than six months old when he established the Denison Arctic Ice Co. He also came up with an idea that he was certain would make both railroad and ranching history as McCoy had done in Kansas a few years earlier.

M. M. Scholl, the "Snake Editor," who wrote much about Denison's early days. Later he was a justice of the peace.

— Photo by Claud Easterly

How New York Got Fresh Meat from Texas

Rankin believed that he could design a railroad refrigerator car capable of hauling fresh meat over long distances. He took his idea to a New York

Dance halls like this one made Denison a favorite of cowboys trailing cattle to market.

capitalist, F. A. Hyatt, who was willing to take a chance. Together they organized the Quick Meat Transit Co., and Rankin went to work to sell the plan to Denison.

Denison, as pointed out in an earlier chapter, was broke and desperate to get some industry. The citizens responded to Rankin by voting $10,000 in bonds to enable him to build slaughtering pens and packing sheds. Officials of the railroad were ecstatic. The Katy would load the meat in Denison, haul it to St. Louis, and connections there would speed it to New York.

Rankin turned next to his friend, McCoy. He urged him to move to Texas and help Denison become another Abilene as a shipping center for cattle. Texas ranchers welcomed the idea of stopping their cattle drives at the Red River — a saving of hundreds of miles and thousands of dollars over trailing them to Kansas. And with the Houston & Texas Central Railroad building north to Denison from Dallas, most Texas cattle could travel by train to the slaughter pens.

By October 1873, Rankin's plant was finished — a huge, sprawling structure covering eight acres just west of the Katy's main line. It began operation on November 26, 1873, when thirty men killed, dressed and readied for shipment 130 head of prime beef. The next day, a little Katy wood-burning locomotive, like the one that had brought the first train into Denison, coupled onto a string of Rankin's new refrigerator cars and started the first leg of the trip to New York.

By this time, Rankin had received more than twenty-four patents on his refrigerator cars and the business was an immediate success. Soon, as many as 300 cattle were being slaughtered and shipped East each day. As the firm became nationally known, Rankin changed its name to the American and Texas Refrigerator Car Company. Meanwhile, McCoy had succeeded in inducing more and more ranchers to bring their cattle to Denison.

However, his dream of making it another Abilene didn't materialize as he had hoped. But in the fall of 1873, more than 1,200 head of live cattle were shipped out of Denison. Many more were slaughtered before being sent to markets.

Success sometimes can plant the seeds of failure. Rankin's refrigerator company lasted only three years, and failed for an unusual reason: its inability to expand. Rankin was not able to show enough profit to attract new capital for such an expansion and was forced to close.

Rankin and McCoy, however, had provided their adopted hometown with a special footnote to history: Denison had become the site of the first successful effort to ship fresh beef to the hungry East. And if McCoy had not quite made it another Abilene, Kansas, Katy's baby did become the principal cowtown in Texas for a little while.

Today Rankin's slaughtering plant is only a memory. But among the weeds and underbrush in the 300 block of East Johnson Street, there is an official Texas historical marker on the site where it stood. It is dedicated not to Rankin, but to Joseph G. McCoy, the man from Illinois who contributed a unique chapter to the history of Denison and of Texas.

"THERE IS A FUTURE FOR THIS CITY – IT WILL BE JUST WHAT WE MAKE IT!

6

Denison, Inc.

"How happy the life unembarrassed by the cares of business."
— Publilius Syrus (42 B.C.), *Maxim* 725

Katy's baby had a business in operation before there were customers to support it.

When a party of sixteen surveyors charting the final course of the Katy Railroad into Texas arrived in what is now Denison on August 19, 1872, John J. Collins and his "refreshment emporium" awaited them. Collins, who hailed from Wyandotte, Kansas, was among the first to seek his fortune in the town the railroad planned to build.

His "bar" was a plank nailed between two trees a few yards east of what now is Forrest Park. Although the surroundings were rustic, the product was quality. Anticipating the influx of home-seekers, Collins had brought in an ample supply of liquors by wagon train. Collins' business flourished from the start. His saloon was the predecessor of as many as fifty-two such watering holes that would make the sale of spiritous liquors the predominant retail business in the new town for several years.

Once the townsite was platted and the first lots sold, Collins' humble saloon was replaced by fancier places, including one of his own. Many offered gambling and female companionship as diversions. It should not be implied, however, that all saloons were dens of iniquity appealing only to the crass. The nicer places, like the Crystal Palace on Main Street, were more on the order of English public houses where leading citizens gathered to lift a glass, visit, or cut a business deal.

There were myriad deals offered, discussed and dismissed. Others were given a brief trial and discarded in failure. A few were opportunities of such potential magnitude that they were embraced, but only after hours of discussion in emporiums like the Crystal Palace.

One dream that came true briefly was to make Denison a military center because of the direct railroad connection it now had with the North and East. Army brass saw some merit in the idea, and in 1873, the Quartermaster Depot at San Antonio's Fort Sam Houston was moved to the new town. It was only a few months, however, before the facility was returned to the Alamo city. Denison never became the defense bastion its leaders hoped it might, but later it built a National Guard Armory and its volunteer guardsmen fought in World Wars I and II. In 1941, a pasture between Denison and Sherman was converted into the Grayson County Basic Flying School, a facility that would grow into Perrin Air Force Base.

When Cotton Was King

With or without the military, Denison's growth seemed assured. The first Katy train had hardly arrived before Rankin had started his center for meat packing and the shipment of cattle. About the same time, local leaders decided to make Denison an important cog in the revolution that was happening in the cotton trade.

Prior to the Civil War, cotton had been the staple of Texas agriculture. In 1860, the state had produced 431,463 bales. By 1870, with farmers still recovering from the war, only 350,628 bales were produced. It was predicted, however, that cotton production would approach a million bales annually over the next decade, and the eyes of New York financiers focused on Denison.

With the Katy Railroad offering direct transportation to St. Louis and the East, Denison was a natural shipping point for cotton growers. This status was enhanced when the Houston & Texas Cen-

When it opened, the Denison Cotton Mill was the largest operation of its kind west of the Mississippi River.
— *Frontier Village Museum Collection*

tral decided in 1873 to make Denison, instead of Red River City, its northern terminus. Now freight from all over Texas could be interchanged at one point, reducing the costs of wagon transport and speeding delivery to markets.

These facts induced Duncan, Sherman & Co., important New York cotton brokers and commission merchants, to build a $20,000 compress near the Katy's Denison tracks. The *Daily News*, never hesitant to point out the superlative advantages of the town, chortled editorially:

"(The compress) will draw to one grand center all the cotton from points tributary to our section. This firm will have abundance of currency in Denison to purchase all of the cotton that comes to market, which they will ship to Liverpool."

Local citizens were even more pleased by a story in the New York *Daily Graphic* of February 5, 1874. That newspaper had sent a woman reporter down to see what was going on in the new town, and she wrote:

"The county seat, Sherman, had been the cotton market for northern Texas, but now that Denison has all of the necessary facilities, King Cotton comes to her in amazing quantities. Some days the Main Street is blocked completely with wagons piled high with the great bales."

Cotton, like the railroads, would remain important to Denison's economy for more than a century. With the compress already a success, a mill to produce fabrics from cotton was not far behind. It came in 1890 when the Denison Cotton Manufacturing Co. erected what then was one of the largest buildings in all of Texas. Denison elementary school pupils for years took pride in the fact that their geography books carried a picture of the structure, labeling it "the largest cotton mill west of the Mississippi."

An impressive structure did not make a successful business, however. Between 1890 and 1905, the company went through a succession of owners. Production was spotty and the mill often was inoperative. A principal backer from the start had been J. T. Munson. A man of many talents, Munson later would survey the West Texas lands the state traded to a contractor for building its capitol in Austin. He was a brother of W. B. Munson, the former Shermanite who had helped the Katy build the town of Denison. In 1904, when it appeared that the operation would not survive, J. T. called on brother Ben for help.

This Munson, who always seemed to be around to rescue Denison from its problems, still believed that a cotton mill could succeed. He attempted to persuade other Denisonians to form a new company to operate the mill, but found no takers. If the plant had failed to succeed after fifteen years, nobody was willing to gamble on another try.

Nobody, that is, except Ben Munson. To get the money to revive the mill, he sold some property between Commerce and Jackson streets in what now is downtown Dallas. Although Munson knew that his Dallas holdings would be worth a fortune in a few years, he was willing to take a future loss if it would help Denison. He incorporated the Denison Cotton Mill Co. on August 5, 1905, with a capital of $150,000 and himself as president. J. R. Handy, a local insurance man, joined him in the project as secretary.

The Cotton Mill Nobody Wanted

From the beginning, Munson didn't want to be saddled with running the mill, and he tried without success to sell stock around the country. Discouraged, he wrote a North Carolina friend: "Do you know of a boom town that would like to have a cotton mill at any old price?"

Unable to sell, he reluctantly decided to run it himself, and it would remain a family operation from then on. In 1908, his son, W. B., Jr., was elected secretary, then became the manager in 1912 and president when his father died. The younger Munson died in 1936 and his sister, Eloise, took over. In 1955, W. B. Munson III was elevated from executive vice-president and treasurer to the presidency.

What some had called "Munson's Folly" in 1904 became one of Denison's largest industries. It had a payroll of more than $1 million and a work force that varied from 300 to 400 people. During World War II, it received an award for the production of critical material for that conflict. Proud employees built homes around the mill south of Denison, and the area became the largest unincorporated community in the state. It was annexed by Denison in the late 1950's.

The State National Bank was a prestigious addition to Main Street.
— *Frontier Village Museum Collection*

Sugar Bottom was Denison's first suburban shopping center.
— *Jenkins Studio Photo*

In the 1930s, horses and wagons outnumbered motor trucks in providing home delivery to customers of the Crystal Ice & Cold Storage Company.
— *Frontier Village Museum Collection*

The W. B. Munson Block on Woodard Street was built in 1888 and still houses a variety of offices.
— *Frontier Village Museum Collection*

By 1977, the Denison Cotton Mill — the largest operation of its kind west of the Mississippi River — fell on hard times again. After almost three-quarters of a century of success, it could no longer compete with foreign imports. It fell to Ben Munson III to close forever the mill his grandfather had sacrificed so much to save.

Finis was written to one of Denison's most historic buildings on the morning of October 19, 1981, when the four-story mill was leveled by fire.

"They Went That-A-Way"

The cotton mill was only one of many once prominent Denison businesses to disappear with the changing times. Another was the Waples-Platter Grocery Co. which, for eighty-seven years, had the distinction of being the only business older than the town itself. Like Collins' saloon, this food company actually existed before the Denison townsite was even surveyed. It started when Sam Hanna and Joe Owens established a commissary at Colbert's Ferry to feed section forces building the Katy toward Denison.

When lots in the new town were sold, they moved from the ferry landing to a tiny building in the 100 block of East Main. They shipped provisions by ox team into the Indian Territory, and also became dealers in buffalo hides. In 1878, A. F. Platter joined the firm, followed in 1885 by W. B. Waples. The company became one of the largest wholesale grocers in the state. In 1920, it moved its headquarters to Fort Worth, but continued the Denison operation until 1959.

Waples-Platter would have had competition for the title of being the first business in town if the Katy Railroad hadn't been late with freight shipments. The goal of J. P. Leeper and E. H. Lingo was to form the company that would furnish lumber to buyers of the first lots in Denison. Their orders from mills in the East were delayed, however, and it was not until 1873 that the company, known as Lingo-Leeper, could supply customers.

Actually the new town was not entirely dependent on the Katy for its lumber or other supplies. Many such necessities were shipped by steamboat up the Red River to Jefferson, then brought by wagon to Denison.

Still operating on Main, the street where it opened 120 years ago, is the Tone Abstract Company. Harrison Tone had no thought of forming such a company when he arrived from Cleveland, Ohio, in 1872 as the secretary and advance agent of the Denison Town Company. His job was to direct the surveyors in laying out streets and to conduct the sale of lots in the new townsite. Once the lots were sold, however, the Town Company had no further use for his services.

When he discovered that abstracts of title had not been issued by the Town Company, he established an office to perform this service. He also took the time to write a succinct history of Denison's first year that remains today a valuable document in local archives.

Tone's friend and contemporary, Franz Kohfeldt, didn't arrive until 1879. Born of German immigrant parents in Illinois in 1865 and orphaned soon after, he was reared by old friends of his family, the George Brauns. They came to Denison to establish the town's first ice plant, predecessor of the Arctic Ice Company that one day would ship beef in refrigerator cars. Kohfeldt managed the ice and wholesale food business which Braun founded, began an apprenticeship in Tone's abstract office and later opened his own real estate business. Kohfeldt & Son Real Estate still operates from the original address — 118 West Main.

Kohfeldt's realty company was involved in helping to locate the site for a business that would evolve into a group of chain stores to be headquartered in Denison. In 1920, Floyd and Jess Babcock acquired a small gasoline service station that specialized in vulcanizing damaged tires. Later they began selling new tires and accessories for Model T Fords. The business grew into a chain of twenty-three outlets in Texas known as the Babcock Bros. Auto Supply Stores.

There were many others on the honor roll of early Denison businesses. In 1899, N. Marsico, a native of Italy, established the Denison Mattress Factory that operated for more than half a century. The J. W. Madden Department Store, Newsom's, and Freel's for years served the clothing needs of Denisonians from prime locations on Main Street. C. J. McManus, who founded Dad & Lad's Store here and expanded it into a chain, even operated an outlet on Guadalcanal when he was stationed there by the navy during World War II.

Two other men's shops had historic importance. The U.S. Clothing Store, established in Denison's very early days by E. Regensburger, operated for well over half a century. James Boyd's Store for Men and Boys is remembered for its slogan painted on barns for miles around, reading: "No clothing fits like ours."

A favorite in the days of the Great Depression was the Witz Bargain Store in the 200 block of West Main. Thousands walked through its bright orange front to buy overalls priced as low as forty-nine cents a pair and shoes for eighty-nine cents.

One business still operated by the same family is the Snow White Laundry. Founded in 1922 by the late Luther Cherry, it is still owned and managed by his son, Bob. The younger Cherry is a former mayor of Denison.

After 101 years of serving the floral needs of the community, the Denison Greenhouses are still in operation. So is the Bayless-Hall Insurance Co., a relatively new name for a company that began in 1888 as the J. R. Handy Agency.

Ashburn's Ice Cream, which started here in 1907, is still known in North Texas. Indeed, it was the forerunner of a series of businesses that have kept Denison in the forefront as a producer of dairy products.

An Island of Cheese?

In 1929, anybody who knew anything about the dairy business would tell you that cheese could never be made successfully in Texas.

In the first place, most of the cattle raised in Texas were intended for slaughter and meat-packing had become a sizeable industry. The few dairy farms existed only to provide milk for local consumption. Almost all of the plants that manufactured cheese and other table products made from milk were located in the North, where there were large dairy herds. It was thought that the hot climate in the South, and Texas in particular, did not lend itself to this kind of industry.

Fifteen years earlier, however, a visionary whose capital consisted of one horse, one delivery wagon and one room from which to operate, decided to experiment with making a variety of cheese products. His name was J. L. Kraft. Success was almost immediate, and by 1929, the Kraft Cheese Co. was ready to gamble that Texas could become an important dairy center. Denison was chosen as the headquarters for his Southwestern Division.

In the beginning, Kraft didn't have to build a plant. Earlier another visionary, John Sherman Knaur, had started such a facility in the 800 block of South Austin Avenue. Unlike Kraft, however, his venture into cheese-making had failed and the Chicago company purchased it. From that beginning, Kraft soon expanded, taking over an abandoned cotton oil mill in northwest Denison and converting it into one of the country's most modern cheese plants. The operation continued to grow with the opening of small bulk cheese manufacturing units in seven other North Texas towns, and distribution centers in San Antonio and Houston. Later Kraft operations in Arkansas, Kansas, Missouri and Oklahoma were placed under the Southwestern Division, and Denison became nationally known as a center for the production of dairy foods.

Like many success stories, this one would not have a happy ending, at least for Denison. In the late 1940's, the federal government offered Kraft a war surplus plant in Garland. It was a larger facility and better suited to the operation than was the Denison complex, and the company moved. All was not lost, however. Almost as Kraft was leaving, the Safeway grocery chain moved one of its subsidiaries into the plant. Soon another followed. More land was purchased, additional facilities installed and today Safeway's Brookside Manufacturing Division remains one of the city's important industries.

Like Kraft, however, there are other familiar business names that are gone but not forgotten. They include the Esler Paint & Paper Co., founded in 1879 by W. M. Esler, Chris Waltz Electric, which opened in 1883, and Kingston's Drug Store, started by C. D. Kingston in 1892. The latter was famous for years as having the only accurate thermometer in town. (In reporting weather conditions, the newspaper always gave the high and low temperature reading "courtesy of Kingston's thermometer.")

One of Denison's most unusual manufacturing companies closed in 1991 after sixty-nine years of worldwide operations. The W. J. Smith Wood Preserving Company had started in 1922 to cut and preserve railroad crossties by injecting a solution of creosote. In the beginning, its primary customer was the Katy Railroad. Later its treated wood products were sold throughout the U.S. and the world. It was estimated that the company, in its years of operation, processed well over 200,000 freight car loads of forest products — enough lumber to build more than 300,000 six-room frame dwellings.

The close of the "tie plant," as it was popularly known, was but another step in the process that has changed Denison from one of the state's most important transportation centers to a city searching for a new economic identity.

An early entrepreneur was John K. Collins, a Kansan who started his business with this open air saloon on September 23, 1872, as bidders gathered to buy the first lots.

— Drawing by H. D. Morgan

7

They Left Their Mark

"I was a stricken deer who left the herd long since."
— William Cowper (1731–1800), *Book III, The Garden*

In the twelve decades since Katy's baby came to life as a new town in Texas, many of those for whom it was either birthplace or adopted home have made names for themselves that won't be soon forgotten. Some loom large in history; others provided only intriguing footnotes. Some "left the herd long since" but never forgot their roots. They deserve attention here, however, because in one guise or another, they left their mark.

When "Taps" Signaled Peace for the World

Hartley Edwards didn't have to blow his own horn to win a unique place in world history. At 11:00 A.M. on November 11, 1918, he raised a $6.25 GI issue bugle to his lips at Tour, France, and blew "Taps" as the official signal that World War I had ended.

In an army that had thousands of buglers, why was this particular rendition by Edwards historic? Because he was the personal bugler of General of the Armies John J. (Blackjack) Pershing. And Pershing himself issued the order to Edwards to use his bugle to tell the world that the armistice had been signed in a railway car in the Compiegne Forest in France.

Nevertheless Edwards almost missed his chance to be a footnote to history. When a sergeant told him to blow "Taps" at eleven o'clock in the morning, he demurred, pointing out that this call was played only at funerals or for "lights out."

"It's an order from General Pershing," he was told.

So Edwards, standing by an old box car, lifted his Conn bugle to his lips and followed the order. He did not learn until later that his "Taps" was Pershing's way of announcing that the lights had gone on again all over the world.

Edwards, the eldest of thirteen children born to an Ellis County farm family, got to be the nation's most famous bugler by accident. He had played a tuba in the Italy, Texas, high school band. So when he joined the army and was sent to Camp Cody, New Mexico, this talent was duly noted by his company commander. He needed a bugler and Edwards got the job.

He had never tooted one before, but he learned quickly and well. So well that when he arrived in France and General Pershing called for a personal bugle corps, Edwards was one of thirty-five who got the assignment. Soon he was the lead musician and, as such, was known as the personal bugler of the commander-in-chief.

After his discharge from the army on October 1, 1919, Edwards moved to Denison, married Irene Graham and became an oiler for the Katy Railroad. He did not give up his bugle, however.

He was named the official bugler for the World War I Veterans. He marched in parades and often played for the Veterans of Foreign Wars, American Legion, Disabled American Veterans and other organizations of former service personnel. Twice he blew "Taps" at Arlington Cemetery in Washington when Presidents Harry Truman and John F. Kennedy laid wreaths on the tomb of the Unknown Soldier.

On July 14, 1919, as the American Expeditionary Forces were heading home, Edwards stood under the Arc de Triomphe in Paris and blew "Taps" for thousands of cheering French gathered to celebrate the victory. As the ceremonies ended, the great general, Ferdinand Foch, turned to Persh-

Hartley Edwards and his bugle sounded taps on November 11, 1918, to signal officially the end of World War I.
— Photo courtesy of Dixie Edwards Klein

ing and said he hoped that the men could come back to France one day.

In 1956, Edwards did. He was invited by President Charles de Gaulle to sound "Taps" once again under the famous victory arch. More than 50,000 cheered as the last notes faded away.

On November 14, 1978 — sixty years and three days after he signaled the end of the war — Edwards died. Eight years before, he had given his old bugle to the Smithsonian in Washington, where it is displayed today. He was not without an instrument, however. The Conn Music Co. made an exact replica of Edwards' original horn, had it plated with gold and presented it to him. Each morning until illness forced him into a nursing home, he roused his neighbors in Denison by tooting "Reveille," the traditional wake-up call of the military.

A Just Dessert

Sweets, not sweet music, were the love of Joseph A. Euper. He moved to Denison in 1875 dreaming of making a living from a small ice cream parlor he opened in the 100 block of West Main. It was a success from the start, and by 1895, he had an even larger emporium at 228 West Main. Euper, however, was not satisfied.

A practical businessman, he knew that selling even large quantities of ice cream and soda water could never match the profitability of neighboring saloons like the White Elephant and the Crystal Palace. What he needed was a new product, and he began serious experimentation at his fountain. And one day, probably by accident, he concocted a combination of ice cream, fruit flavoring, and sparkling water.

No picture of Joseph A. Euper has been found, but this drug store might have been the one in Denison where he invented one of the nation's most popular drinks.

— *Chamber of Commerce*

The result was the ice cream soda. After more than a century, the drink is still so popular that one Michigan town honors its inventor annually with a "Joseph A. Euper Day."

Apparently the creamy concoction so loved by Americans never brought Euper much money. In 1906, he closed his confectionary and moved to California to sell real estate. He died there in 1937 at the age of eighty-seven.

The Rajah

One day in 1915, Bob Connery, scout for the St. Louis National Club, dropped off from a Katy passenger train in Denison where the obscure Western Association fielded a baseball team. At the game that afternoon, he noted with interest a kid playing shortstop for the Denison club.

The fellow didn't look so hot in the field. On looking up his batting figures, Connery saw that he was batting only .277 against Class C bush-league pitching and had hit only .232 the year before. Also, he had been let out by both Dallas and Hugo, Oklahoma, as not worthy of further trial.

Nevertheless the scout figured that he was a natural hitter who wasn't hitting because of the wild pitching — that he probably would be a whiz at bat against good pitchers. He bought him for St. Louis for $500.

His name was Rogers Hornsby, called by many the greatest right-hand hitter in the history of baseball. He was a big league star for sixteen years and was the leading batter in the National League for seven of those years. After his playing career, he managed five different major league clubs. He also is remembered as one of the most controversial characters in baseball history

"The Rajah," as sportswriters dubbed him,

spent a total of twenty-two years in the major leagues before being traded to minors in 1938.

Hornsby was not a native of Denison. However, one of his two sons, Rogers Jr., grew up there and graduated from Denison High School in 1937. He was killed in World War II. Rogers Sr., died in 1963 and is buried near Austin at Hornsby Bend, named for his historic ancestor, Reuben Hornsby.

"Hello Central, Give Me a Line"

Denison can't claim to be the birthplace of the telephone. However, it was a Katy communications department employee in Denison who was destined to revolutionize Alexander Graham Bell's invention. Bell patented his first crude machine to transmit voices in 1877 and scientists continued to work on improving its quality. But it was not until 1930 that a Denisonian developed a device that would expand telephone use many times over.

His name was Carlos F. Johanning and he finished only the first four grades of school in his native Richmond, Indiana. But he had a natural bent toward mechanics and eventually became a telephone technician for the Katy Railroad. He was headquartered on the second floor of the Union Station along with train and crew dispatchers, the division superintendent and his staff and half a hundred others needed to keep the railroad operating.

The telephone had become almost as vital as the telegraph as a communications tool for the railroad. No longer was it necessary to send messages by tapping them out in Morse code. With the telephone, one needed only to dial a number and talk to another individual in the next office or thousands of miles away. Thus one of Johanning's first assignments was to install the first automatic telephone system in the railroad's general offices in Dallas in 1912.

Although messages now could be sent directly and quickly by voice, there was one drawback. The individual answering the call had no way to transfer it to a different office or to summon another person who was remote from the instrument. Johanning set out to solve that problem.

To the standard telephone base, he added another. The auxiliary base was wired to receive incoming calls, but it had a second feature: There were four push buttons, each controlling an electrical circuit that could be wired to another instrument. The buttons were switches that allowed calls to be transferred to another telephone in the same office or even on another floor.

Carlos F. Johanning built kiddie cars, false teeth, and invented a new phone.

— Photo courtesy of Julia Johanning

Johanning's model of the first push button telephone attracted national attention in communication circles. On December 2, 1930, he was issued a patent. The Katy, however, had a policy that any new ideas or inventions developed by employees were the property of the railroad. For designing and producing a device that improved telephone use all over the world, Johanning received only letters of thanks from Katy officials and a check for $200.

The telephone company that bought the invention from the Katy (what it paid isn't known) graciously sent Johanning a gold-plated model.

The push button telephone was Johanning's only invention. When he retired from the Katy in 1940 and moved to Dallas, however, he began a new and gummy career.

He made false teeth for dentists!

The Trip That Changed a Life

Johanning's push button telephone was not even an idea in his mind when his son, Douglass,

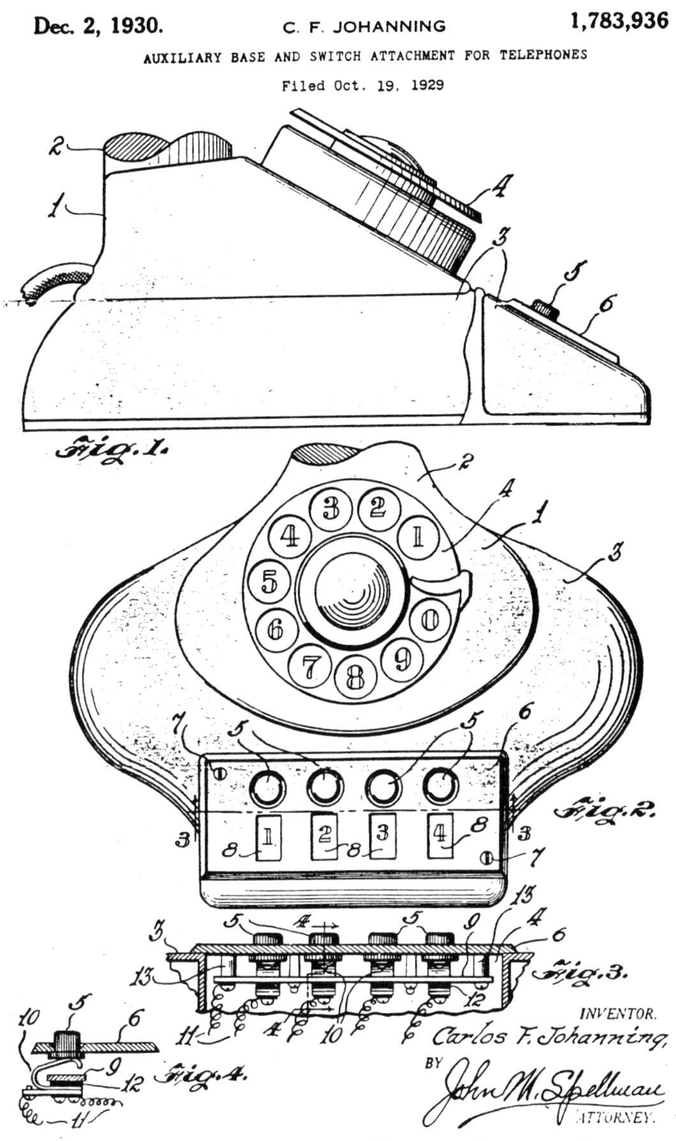

Dec. 2, 1930.
C. F. JOHANNING
1,783,936
AUXILIARY BASE AND SWITCH ATTACHMENT FOR TELEPHONES
Filed Oct. 19, 1929
Fig. 1.
Fig. 2.
Fig. 3.
Fig. 4.
INVENTOR.
Carlos F. Johanning
BY
ATTORNEY.

This telephone patented by a Katy employee made one instrument do the work of several.
— *Photo courtesy of Julia Johanning*

was born in Dallas a few years before the family moved to Denison. But the proud father dreamed that one day the boy would grow up to share his own interest in technology and possibly choose a career with the Katy or another railroad.

Things might have happened that way if the Dallas *Morning News* editors hadn't decided to send a youngster to Washington on November 11, 1921, to place a wreath on the new grave of the Unknown Soldier. From the thousands of youngsters in Dallas, they chose two-year-old Douglass Johanning.

From the day he toddled out to the fresh crypt in Arlington Cemetery and laid a wreath larger than his full height on the burial site of the World War I hero "known only to God," his life would never be the same again.

It wasn't that he had a vivid memory of the event. But in his years of growing up in Denison, he realized that he had been an actor in a brief, but important, moment on history's stage. Douglass dreamed that one day he would return to Arlington and visit the single grave that is a memorial to all of America's war dead.

The opportunity came when he was fifteen. Along with Jack Heimburger and Murray Marshall, fellow Boy Scouts, he rode the Katy to Washington for his pilgrimage. This time, while standing at the tomb where he had laid a wreath thirteen years before, young Johanning took a vow. He decided to devote his life to seeing to it that there would never be another Unknown Soldier.

He became a mortician. And as soon as World War II began, he enlisted and became a sergeant in the American Graves Registration Service. By the summer of 1943, he was in the jungles of New Guinea. His unit was unique. Each man, including the officers, was a licensed mortician and embalmer. They usually worked alone, driving their own Jeeps, cooking their own food and scouting the battlefields for the dead. Their goal: to find all soldiers killed in action, identify and bury them. Johanning's group also had the responsibility to embalm and bury those who died in field hospitals.

Although Johanning and his colleagues did not find every soldier killed in action and provide a proper burial, the work of the American Graves Registration Service was recognized and praised all around the world. In 1945, when Prime Minister John Curtin of Australia died, a call went out to Douglass Johanning in the jungle. He was asked to fly to Canberra and embalm the body of that country's leader.

After the war, Johanning returned to Dallas but not the funeral business. He devoted the rest of his life to working with non-profit organizations, including the Dallas Community Chest and the Lighthouse for the Blind.

Franz' Town

Franz Kohfeldt's interest was not death, but creating a new and better life for others. His dream was to build cities.

Kohfeldt moved to Denison as a youngster in 1879, the orphan son of German parents, and Katy's town remained his home until his death in 1938. Except for the realty company that still bears his name, there is no memorial to him in his home town. But in Texas City, more than 350 miles from Denison as the crow flies, there is a Franz Kohfeldt High School. It stands in honor of the man whose vision helped to turn a flat wasteland covered with salt grass into a petro-chemical center known around the world.

Kohfeldt was a twenty-five-year-old apprentice in the abstract office of Harry Tone in 1890 when he conceived of building a metropolis on the Texas coast. He had gone to Sherman on business when he accidentally encountered a French engineer then stationed in Baltimore. Always interested in meeting new people, Kohfeldt began a conversation with the visitor. The incident would set his life on a new course and change the history of the Texas coast.

In their casual meeting, the Baltimore visitor mentioned that he had learned in Washington that the government was planning to build a deep-water port on the Gulf coast at a place called Shoal Point. Houston was then a small inland town, and nearby Galveston's port was too small to handle the growth of shipping that Texas' growing economy would demand.

"Such a project would make that port the New York of Texas someday," Kohfeldt told his new friend. The engineer agreed.

The young clerk couldn't get this potential out of his thoughts. He pictured such a port in his mind, and the attendant warehouses, factories, railroads and residences that would support it. He decided to acquire some land around Shoal Point before this planned development became public.

Young Kohfeldt had no ready cash, but was able to borrow $500. He boarded a Katy train and rushed to the coast. Once at Shoal Point, he discovered that optioning the land was easy. The owners considered the property almost worthless. For $500 Kohfeldt was given the right to buy up to 10,000 acres. Meanwhile some Minnesota capitalists had bought the settlement itself for development.

It was slow, but there was some progress. By 1893, the population had grown to 300, the town had a post office and was named Texas City.

Franz Kohfeldt was a German orphan who envisioned a port as important as New York on the Texas coast.
— *Denison Herald photo*

Dredging began on an eight-foot channel and a four-mile rail line was built to connect with the Gulf, Colorado & Santa Fe. There was still little interest in Kohfeldt's property, however, and he struggled to keep the taxes paid and his option intact. Eventually he was able to sell 3,000 acres of his land.

Although Texas City now calls itself the "Port of Opportunity," not much of this brag was evident in the town before World War II. In 1936, two years before Franz Kohfeldt died, the population was only 3,534.

He did not live to see Texas City acquire oil and sugar refineries, petro-chemical plants, the largest tin smelter in America and other industries. Even with all of this, however, the town never achieved Kohfeldt's dream that it would become "the New York of Texas." Of Texas' twenty-seven seaports, however, Texas City is now the third largest, ranking behind Houston and Corpus Christi in total tonnage. Franz Kohfeldt would be as proud of "his" town today as it is of him 101 years after he "discovered" it.

The B-17 Pilot That Could

Ask any pilot who flew heavy bombers in World War II and they'll tell you that what twenty-four-year-old Bill Lawley did couldn't be done.

But 1st Lt. William R. Lawley did it, so Denison, Texas, Leeds, Alabama, and Perrin Field all claim him as their top hero. For his indomitable courage, he received the nation's highest military decoration — the Medal of Honor.

Lawley was born in Alabama, but he got his basic flight training at Perrin Field. And he married a Denison girl, Amelia Dodd, daughter of a Katy locomotive engineer. Although they now live in Lawley's native state, both claim close ties to Denison.

His story begins on February 20, 1944. Lawley was flying his tenth mission over the death-ridden skies of Germany that day. He had reached his target, Leipzig, but his B-17 had dropped only part of its bomb load. His plane still carried 5,000 pounds of explosives which could not be dropped because of frozen release mechanisms, and he was returning to base with his formation.

He was just inside Belgium when some twenty enemy fighters suddenly swooped down, pouring a steady stream of bullets and 20mm shells on his hapless Flying Fortress. A mortar struck his co-pilot, killing him instantly. Other shells shattered one engine, much of the controls, the radio and the interphone. Bucket-size holes were blown in the wings, the nose, right waist section, tail wheel area and the right cockpit windshield. The co-pilot's blood completely covered the rest of the glass, blocking out Lawley's vision. Lawley himself was bleeding about the face and arms from cuts made by the flying glass.

Slowed by the damage and the heavy bomb load, the B-17 was left to its fate by the rest of the formation. Lawley ordered the crew to bail out and the engineer did. Then another crew member reported that the two gunners were severely wounded and couldn't move, so Lawley elected to keep flying. He clung desperately to the controls with one

Col. William Lawley, aviation hero of World War II and recipient of the Medal of Honor.
— *Photo courtesy of William Lawley*

hand. With the other, he held up the headless body of his co-pilot which had slumped over, jamming the right controls. He called in the bombadier to help.

Nose heavy, all tabs shot out and minus a motor, the Fortress was alone. No formation. No escort.

To bring up the nose, Lawley wrapped both arms around the controls and yanked backward with all of his strength. At the same time, he stomped the left rudder with both feet to bring up a dangerously low right wing. It worked.

Enemy fighters attacked again, but by masterful evasive action, he managed to lose them. When another engine caught fire, he extinguished it with skillful flying. Refusing first aid, he finally passed out from shock and loss of blood. The bombadier revived him.

Over France, Lawley had thought of trying to

jetsam his bomb load. He rejected the idea because the undercast was heavy and he feared that the deadly projectiles might fall on French civilians. Coming over the English coast, another engine ran out of fuel and had to be feathered. A second engine started to burn and continued to do so until he crash landed the B-17 on a British field. Lawley, his arms half paralyzed and his body cut by flying glass, stumbled from the plane and collapsed from exhaustion.

Now retired, Col. and Mrs. Lawley live in Birmingham, Alabama.

Three Brothers Who Counted

Munson is a name that has been synonymous with Denison since before the townsite was even selected. It is also a name known throughout the world, thanks to three brothers from Illinois, who came to Texas in the 1870's and each of whom achieved success in different areas.

One, William Benjamin Munson, Sr., would help to found Denison, build railroads, operate the largest cotton mill west of the Mississippi and eventually own ten million acres of Texas ranches and farm land.

J. T. Munson, like his brother, Ben, was educated as a surveyor. He is best remembered by history as the landsman chosen to survey the 3,050,000 acres of West Texas lands that the state traded to a contractor in exchange for building the magnificent capitol in Austin. J. T., the bachelor Munson, also was a partner with his older brother in the real estate business, in the Southern Railroad and Con-

The three brothers whose names are synonymous with the birth, growth and development of Denison — J. T., William G., and Thomas Volney Munson.

— *Denison Herald photo*

struction Company, the Denison & Washita Valley Railroad, the Cotton Mill and other corporations.

The third brother, Thomas Volney Munson, had few interests beyond the science of horticulture. Today he is remembered throughout the world as the greatest viticulturist in history.

Thus it is not surprising that the family name is everywhere. In Denison, Munson is, and always has been, the best known name. There is a Munson Street, a Munson Stadium and a beautiful Munson Park. Since the town's beginning, there always has been a Munson among the local business and civic leaders. As this is written, William Benjamin Munson IV (Ben Four to his friends) is the mayor.

In Rockwall County, there is a town of Munson (population 64) that sprang up on what was once a ranch owned by Ben I. The Denison Public Library is housed on what was once the site of the W. B. Munson, Sr. home. Principal architect of the W. B. Munson Foundation, established in the 1940's, was Eloise Munson, daughter of Ben I. The Foundation has given substantial support over the years to hospitals, schools, playgrounds and especially the Library.

However, the most valuable (to historians) of W. B. Munson's papers are not in the Denison Library. They are at the Panhandle Plains Historical Society Museum in Canyon. So is the headquarters house of Munson's historically famed T-Anchor Ranch which, in the 1870's, spread over the present townsite of Amarillo and considerably beyond. Miss Eloise gave the collection and house to the Canyon museum in 1966 because that is the area most important, next to Denison, in her father's land, banking, industrial and railroad empire.

While brothers Ben I and J. T. were concentrating their efforts on business, T. V. was satisfied with being what he described as "a horticulturist and nurseryman." When he came to Texas in the late 1870's and planted his first grapevines on a two-acre plot north of town, he had no idea that one day he would gain world fame by saving the French wine industry.

Although the French gave him the Legion of Honor for his work, they still don't like to admit that there's a taste of Texas in every glass of French wine. However, whether it's a vintage Burgundy or this year's Bordeaux, wines from any of the vineyards in the south of France trace their ancestry to vines that once grew in the Red River Valley near

The grave of T. V. Munson, the great horticulturist, in Fairview Cemetery is marked by a grapevine carved in stone.
— *Photo by John Clift*

Denison.

By 1893, Munson was growing some 300 varieties of Texas grapes. One of their outstanding characteristics was their resistance to *phylloxera*, a root disease that often destroys entire vineyards. That same year, he was asked to arrange the most complete grape genus ever compiled and show it at the Colombian Exposition in Chicago.

Meanwhile *phylloxera* had spread throughout France and it appeared that the wine industry was doomed. But when French experts saw the Munson display in Chicago, it gave them a glimmer of hope. They asked him to send root stock to France. There every vineyard was grafted with cuttings from Munson's grapes and they miraculously survived. French wines have had a taste of Texas since.

When Munson died, his family erected over his grave a granite shaft with a grapevine carved in the stone. His vineyards were given to Texas A&M University where, for reasons never satisfactorily explained, they were destroyed.

Fortunately, they are now being restored on the grounds of Grayson County College. In 1977, a grant was given by the W. B. Munson Foundation to establish the T. V. Munson Memorial Vineyard there. A worldwide search was started to find as many varieties of Munson grapes as possible. More than one hundred had been discovered by 1991. In 1988, the T. V. Munson Viticulture and Ecology Center and Museum opened.

The Munson name will be honored for generations to come.

The Fighting Irishman

Unlike the Munson brothers, the bouncing baby boy born on August 15, 1880, to Daniel O'Reilly, a likeable stonemason, and his red-headed wife, Mary Synott, did not stay in Denison to make his fortune.

In retrospect, the birth of Edward S. O'Reilly should have been an occasion for feasting and celebrating with rounds of drinks at the Palace Bar or at Pat Lowry's California Saloon on Crawford. "Tex" O'Reilly, as the youngster would be known to the world, would become one of the most colorful personages ever to call Denison home.

His father's talent lay in turning stone into beautiful buildings, but Edward O'Reilly wanted to write. He would become internationally famous as a soldier of fortune, writer and lecturer.

O'Reilly got his education between stints of soldiering and newspaper jobs. At eighteen, he was with the American forces fighting the Spanish-American War in Cuba and the Philippines. He took time off to marry Sophia Blakeney, daughter of a San Saba rancher, then embarked on a newspaper and military career that would take him to San Antonio, St. Louis and eventually all over the world.

At one time, he was managing editor of the San Antonio *Light,* then moved on to the same job with the *Herald-News* in Joliet, a Chicago suburb. Later he became a roving correspondent for the Associated Press in Chicago and Mexico. In 1901 and 1902, he was in China as a drill instructor for the Chinese Imperial Army. By 1913, he was an officer in the Mexican Army. In 1918, he was back in Texas as a major in the national guard.

Throughout his life, O'Reilly wrote magazine articles and books and lectured about his experiences. And while he never returned to Denison to live, it always had a special place in his heart.

He Went Down Shooting

Neither Fred W. Wilson nor Sam Pattillo were writers, lecturers or soldiers of fortune. They were fighting men who were the first from Denison to die in battle for their country — Wilson in World War I and Pattillo in World War II. The Denison American Legion Post is named in their honor.

Except for some trouble with his airplane, Sam Pattillo might have been at Pearl Harbor on December 7, 1941. Pattillo and his crew were at Hamilton Field, California, on December 6, planning to start their flight across the Pacific that night. Pattillo's younger brother, James, also an Air Corps second lieutenant and flight instructor, was there, too, but only to say goodbye.

With the destruction of Pearl Harbor, Pattillo and his crew were held in California until they could be deployed elsewhere. In mid-December, they were sent to the Far East. On January 16, 1942, on a mission from Java to bomb Japanese shipping in Menado Bay, they were attacked by nine Japanese fighters, lost two engines and limped back to Kendari, Celebes, to repair their plane. However, with Japanese ground forces approaching, they destroyed the craft and caught a ride back

Sam Pattillo, first Denisonian to die in World War II.
— Photo courtesy Judge James Pattillo

to Java.

On February 8, with a different plane, they took off to bomb the airfield at Kendari (which had been theirs until a few days earlier when the Japanese captured it). Because of an undercast, they flew over a Japanese aircraft carrier without being aware of it (they had no radar). The carrier was aware of them, however, and launched its fighters. They attacked the lead plane piloted by Lt. Pattillo, and the co-pilot of the plane on their left wing watched as their leader went down. There were no survivors.

Sam Pattillo had turned twenty-three the previous September. The U.S. had been at war two months and one day. Denison had lost its first son to die in World War II. There would be many others.

The Story That Even the Navy Wouldn't Believe

As war records go, that of E. J. (Buddy) Wagner of Denison is unique.

He may be the only pilot in U.S. Navy history to "scare" an enemy bomber into crashing without firing a shot, and sink a 38,000-ton battleship with a single bomb.

For the first incident, he got derisive hoots until investigation proved him right. For the other, he received the Navy Cross, second only to the Medal of Honor as a decoration for valor.

In 1942, the U.S. had just begun its first major offensive in the South Pacific. Lt.(jg) Wagner was piloting a tiny, antiquated, pontooned biplane that had been catapulted off the deck of a cruiser an hour earlier. The fabric-covered plane was moving along 500 feet off the surface of the ocean near Turk

E. J. (Buddy) Wagner "scared" a Japanese bomber into crashing and later sank an enemy battleship with one bomb.
— Photo courtesy of E. J. Wagner

Island. He was looking for Japanese shipping. Glancing back over his shoulder, he was startled to see a Japanese medium bomber bearing down on him.

"There was only one thing to do . . . and I did it," he recalls.

He headed for the water. The bomber stayed on his tail, trying to get its nose guns to bear. Wagner cranked his flaps down as far as they would go and he began circling about five feet above the water at a snail-like twenty-eight knots.

The Japanese pilot slowed down also and tried to follow the maneuver. Apparently he was so intent on shooting down his prey that he forgot to watch his air speed. He smashed the plane into the Pacific and oily black smoke began to rise. Wagner watched as sharks converged on the wreckage.

Back on the ship, the commander couldn't believe the story and dispatched a destroyer to check it out. The bomber was still floating and the sailors who went aboard found a map in the dead pilot's pocket. It showed an airfield that the U.S. had never heard of.

"We blasted that field the next day," Wagner recalls.

It was another incident that resulted in his being awarded the Navy Cross. This time, he was flying from a carrier and leading a formation of four dive bombers in search of the Japanese Battleship *Hyuga*. Each of the divers carried a 2,000-ton bomb.

The ship and the bombers spotted each other at almost the same instant. At 15,000 feet, the planes started their dive and the ship's guns began firing. Wagner says that "ack-ack was bursting in different colors — red, blue, black — and we had to dodge between them."

With his right hand on the stick, thumbing the red button that sent 50-caliber bullets from his wing machine gun to the deck below, Wagner used his left hand to release the bomb bay doors. The projectile slid part way out of the plane's belly, armed and waiting, while the gunner tossed out strips of tinfoil to jam the Japanese radar. Then he punched the stud that released the bomb.

The gunner had taken some shrapnel in the leg and Commander Wagner hauled back on the controls. Under the high-gee strain, this caused his blood to leave the brain momentarily and he experienced what was known as a temporary "red out." Finally he got the plane on keel and headed back to the carrier 200 miles away. The bomber was damaged beyond repair and was tossed over the side after it landed.

When he was safely aboard the ship, he learned that his plane had scored the only hit. The armor-piercing bomb had struck amidship, almost going down the smokestack. When it exploded, so did the boilers. The great battleship rolled over and sank.

Only then did Wagner realize the date. It was July 28 — his mother's birthday.

8

Main Lines and Side Tracks

"There has never since been and never again will be a time of such inherent, characteristic romance in railroading."

— Lucius Beebe in *High Iron* (New York: Bonanza Books, 1938)

March 10, 1873, is a day that should loom large in the history of the nation. It doesn't.

Even in Denison, where it all happened, there isn't so much as an historical marker. Yet it was here, at a point off Main Street, where the entire United States was linked by rail for the first time.

Every school student knows the story of how, when the rails of the Union Pacific and those of the Central Pacific were joined at Promotory Point, Utah, on May 10, 1869, celebrities gathered from all over. They came to hear oratory and to drive a golden spike. The linking of the two lines gave America its first railroad connecting the Atlantic and Pacific coasts. It was one of the major events in the history of U.S. transportation.

No such fanfare occurred less than four years later when the first Houston & Texas Central train from the south rolled into the wooden station at the foot of Denison's Main Street at 7:00 P.M. on March 10, 1873. Yet the arrival of the little train was more significant than the event in Utah. The joining of the Central and the Katy at Denison meant that all of the United States — North, South, East and West — were linked for the first time by the steel bands of the railroad.

Most of the hundred or so residents who gathered at the station that evening did not realize the importance of the event. But L. S. Owings, the former governor of Arizona Territory, whom his fellow Denisonians had named as their first mayor, did know. He sent the following telegram to his counterparts in Galveston, Houston, New York, Boston, Chicago, St. Louis and San Francisco:

> Denison, to her sister cities from the Atlantic to the Pacific, sends greetings:
> "It has remained for Denison to become the great connecting link uniting the South with the East, North and West. May the union be one of lasting peace and prosperity."

Mayor Owings read his telegram to the assembled crowd and saluted the engineer and crew of the train. There were no other formalities.

After a few minutes, the engineer tooted the locomotive's weak little whistle and moved on toward Red River City, the hamlet the H&TC still planned as its terminus. The crowd dispersed, proud that Denison now had two railroads. However, most were still unaware that they had been present at a unique moment in history when a great nation was joined for the first time by rail.

For a short time, the Central continued to drop off freight for transfer to the Katy at its Denison station. Passenger trains, however, went on to Red River City. Travelers hoping to make connections with Katy trains had to be transported the four miles back to Denison by stage or wagons. This was an inconvenience, and later in March, all Central trains began stopping at the Katy depot. Soon other rail lines would be using the same station.

Mail By Mule

Denison was the ideal location, geographically, for a transportation center. Chickasaw Ben Colbert's ferry had provided an important crossing of the Red River long before the Katy Railroad built its bridge across the stream. When the Butterfield Overland Mail began hauling passengers from St. Louis to San Francisco on September 15, 1858, it crossed into Texas on Colbert's boats and made a rest stop at Sand Springs in what is now the southwest side of Denison. When that service stopped on

March 14, 1861, after Texas joined the Confederacy, scheduled mail and transportation to the area was suspended for the duration of the Civil War.

Communications, however, were not totally cut off. A rider on a Mexican mule came each week from Fort Worth, via Denton and Sherman, to bring mail to Colbert's Ferry and the struggling settlement there. Freight wagons continued their trek from Texas into the Indian Territory, usually stopping for water and relaxation at Sand Springs.

Once the Katy and H&TC were operating trains into the young town of Denison, there was a new need for supporting transportation. By January 1873, regular stage lines were operating between Fort Worth and Denison. In February 1873, Mayor Owings himself started a stage line to Bonham and another to Whitesboro and Gainesville. Each of these helped boost the economic boom brought on by the coming of the railroads.

And more were on the way.

Here Come the Trains

Railroad mania gripped the town and new lines were planned in all directions. Between 1877 and 1895, five more railroads would fan out from Denison and would be headquartered there. Still others were planned but never built.

In 1876, Robert S. Stevens, the general manager who had built the Katy into Denison, left the company. He did not quit railroading, however, nor did he lose his interest in the town. With his old friend, W. B. Munson, Sr., he planned two more lines originating there. One would be the Denison & Southeastern; the other the Denison & Pacific.

On July 27, 1877, the Denison & Southeastern Railway was chartered by Denison and Greenville citizens to build a line between those two points. A principal financier was the Katy, and both Munson and Stevens were investors. The line was completed in 1879. In 1880, its name was officially changed to the Missouri, Kansas and Texas Extension Railroad Company — a ploy designed to meet stringent Texas laws governing railways.

(In those days, state law required railroad companies operating in Texas to have their headquarters in the state. Thus there were "two" Katys — the principal one headquartered in Missouri and the Texas line which later built system offices in Dallas.)

On April 24, 1878, the Denison and Pacific Railway was chartered with dreams of a direct route to California. Within two years, forty-two miles had been built to Gainesville. It was operated by the Katy and its Texas Extension Railway Company until 1891 when it was sold to the Missouri, Kansas & Texas Railway of Texas. The same year, Katy of Texas made the Denison and Southeastern a part of its system. Later it became a segment of the main line between Denison and Dallas.

Meanwhile Munson decided to build a railroad of his own. On January 8, 1886, he and others incorporated the Denison and Washita Valley (D&WV). Their hope was to extend the line eventually to Denver, Colorado, and tap the rich coal fields of Oklahoma on the way. Less than seven miles were built in Texas — from Denison to the Red River, where it connected with the Katy's main line north to Atoka, Oklahoma. From Atoka, the D&WV built another fifteen miles to Coalgate and thus did tap a major coal field in the Sooner State. In 1892, the Katy took over that operation and finally purchased it in 1903.

Everybody Loved Nellie

Except for the Denison and Southeastern to Greenville, all of Denison's new railroads headed north or west. This may have inspired the chartering on January 27, 1887, of the Denison, Bonham & New Orleans (DB&NO).

By 1901, it had not yet completed its line to Bonham and was out of funds. The Katy had it rechartered and completed laying rails into that Fannin County seat. It was operated by that railroad until 1923, when it was sold to Bonham purchasers.

The fame of the DB&NO lay in the daily passenger train it operated between Denison and Bonham. Known as "Nellie," the train was hardly deluxe. It was a "mixed" train — that is, passengers and baggage and mail rode in one rickety wooden car. Freight, when there were shipments, went in cars attached to the rear.

Travelers loved the little train's informality on the twenty-eight-mile trip. The late J. E. Maguire, father of the author of this book, was the last regular engineer on the line before it was abandoned in 1929. He recalled how the crew liked to make the trip a pleasant one for passengers. When watermelons were in season, he would halt "Nellie" by a

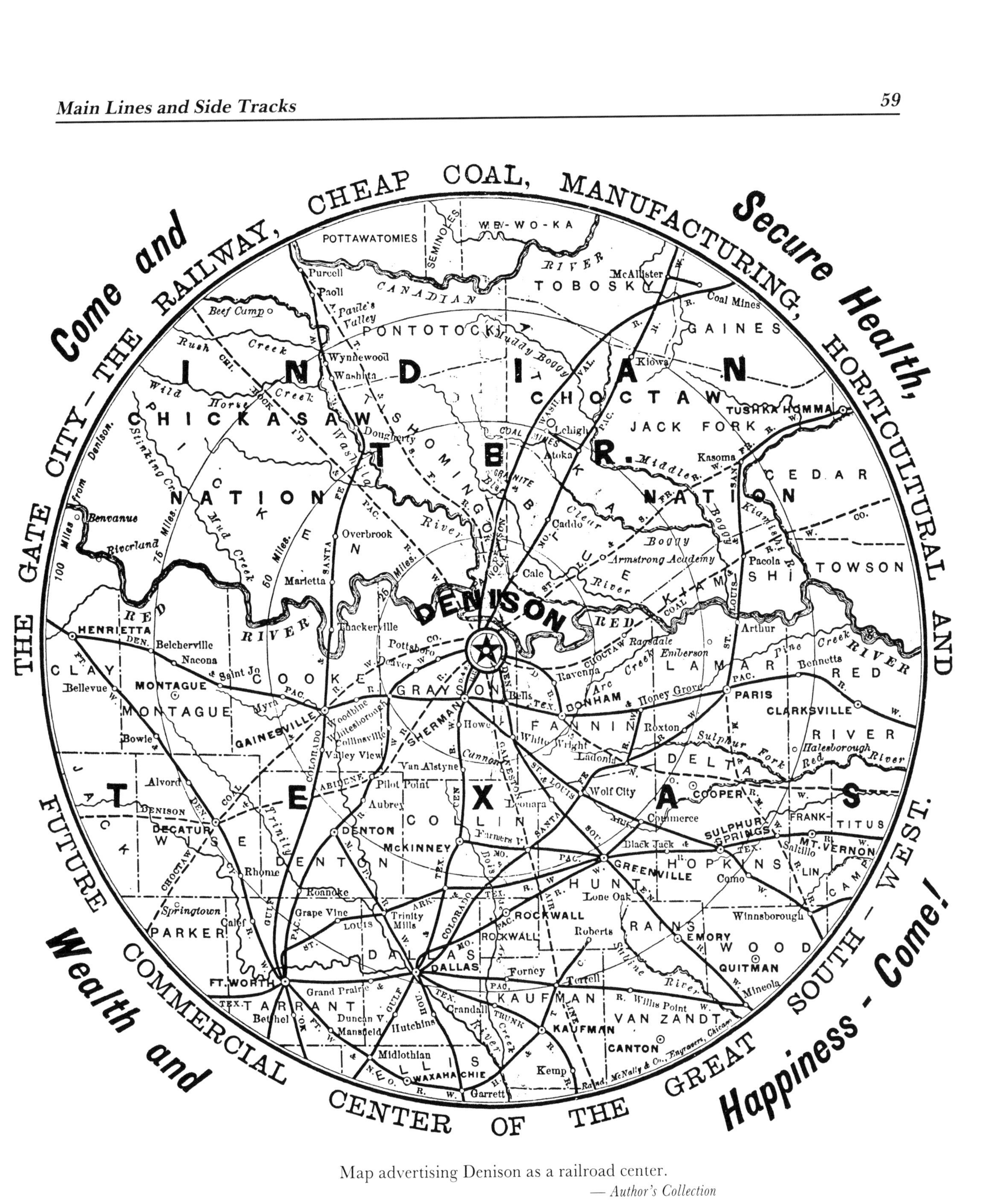

Map advertising Denison as a railroad center.
— Author's Collection

Early photo of Denison's great Union Station with streetcar awaiting the arrival of a train.
— Photo from C. J. McManus Collection

melon patch and everybody would alight and feast awhile.

The last home-spawned railroad was the Denison & Pacific Suburban, chartered on April 18, 1895. It had no connection with the earlier Denison & Pacific Railway Company. The line was a branch of the Texas & Pacific, which had built from Texarkana to Sherman and wanted a connection with the Katy at Denison. The T&P built the seven-mile branch. Later the T&P became a part of the Missouri Pacific, which in turn was merged with the Union Pacific before that system also got control of the Katy. Today all three of these once independent roads are a part of the Union Pacific.

From Lawyer to President

The T&P was never a "major" among the lines serving Denison, but it provided an important transportation link to Texarkana on the eastern edge of the state and El Paso at the far western edge. In the 1950's, J. T. (Tom) Suggs, a prominent Denison lawyer, joined the railroad as its general counsel in Dallas and later became the T&P president. Suggs' father was an early city commission member.

A line that didn't make it beyond the planning stage was the Chocktaw Coal and Railway Company. Financial interests in Arkansas and Minnesota projected the line, but it was never built.

In 1909, the St. Louis and San Francisco Railway crossed the Red River and into Denison. Along with the Katy, it became a major north-south carrier. For many years, the two roads jointly operated the *Texas Special* and *The Bluebonnet,* two of the premier passenger trains between Texas and St. Louis. The Frisco's fast *Black Gold* provided overnight service between Dallas and Tulsa via Denison.

A year after the arrival of the Frisco, the Missouri, Oklahoma & Gulf Railroad was chartered. Its main line extended from Baxter Springs, Kansas, and crossed into Texas east of Denison at Car-

One of America's most famous trains, the Katy's *Texas Special*, served Denison for half a century.
— *Katy Railroad Archives*

One of the nation's first streamliners visited Denison, but was never in regular service through this city.
— *Author's Collection*

penter's Bluff. In 1921, it was renamed the Kansas, Oklahoma & Gulf (KO&G). It later became a part of the Missouri Pacific.

The First Streamliner

Denison, which already could claim to be the terminal for the first railroad to enter Texas from the north, and to be the site where the entire nation was united by rail for the first time, soon would claim another distinction. In 1932, the first streamliner to operate anywhere in the country arrived in Denison.

By today's standards, it wasn't much of a train. But it was a long step forward from the wood-burning steam locomotive that arrived forty years earlier. This one was gasoline-powered, had two cars and ran on rubber tires instead of flanged wheels. It was built for the Texas & Pacific for use between Texarkana and Fort Worth. Touted in advertising as "an epoch in American railroading," the experimental train was not successful and didn't continue in service long. Many ideas embodied in its design and construction, however, were used in later streamliners like the Katy's *Texas Special*.

It was also in Denison that one of the most famous of all safety slogans was coined: *"If you drive, don't drink. If you drink, don't drive."*

It was the creation in the mid-1930's of J. E. Johnston, ticket agent at the Union Station. For years, he wrote safety messages of all kinds and posted a new batch of them each week on the depot bulletin board.

No town in Texas has as many historic ties to trains as does Denison. The railroads not only were the backbone of the economy, but they gave the town a unique lifestyle. The wail of locomotive whistles and the noise of a long freight drag pulling in from the south were sounds as commonplace as the striking of the courthouse clock in a county seat.

As recently as World War II, five steam railroads served Denison. The Katy alone operated eighteen regular passenger trains and the Frisco and KO&G one each. In fact, a total of forty-three passenger-carrying trains were in and out of town daily if one includes the interurbans of the Texas Electric Railway.

Fortunately, Denison can still "hear the train

blow." Although most of the railroads mentioned here have disappeared as entities, enough tracks remain to ensure that Denison will continue as a "main line" town, at least for north-south freights. However, neither the city nor the railroads that served it will ever be the same as they were into the middle of this century.

In fact, the Katy has gone forever. It began as the Union Pacific, Southern Branch, in 1869, and became a part of the Union Pacific again in 1988 when it was merged with that railroad. The merger was the death knell for the company that parented Denison and nurtured it into importance. Gone with the Katy are the great shops that employed hundreds, the freight classification yards that once were among the largest in Texas, and the division offices that filled the upper floors of Union Station. And gone forever is Denison's fame as a railroad center.

Clang, Clang, Clang Went the Trolley

Even the interurban — that unique cross between a streetcar and a conventional train — is gone. It was introduced by Denison to the rest of Texas.

Possibly because of Denison's railroad heritage, its citizens always have had an uncommon interest in transportation. While other developing towns were content with muddy streets and horses for transport, Denison was planning public transit. The town was less than a decade old when the Denison Street Railway was formed and steel rails were laid down the center of Main Street. The wooden coaches, enclosed for passenger comfort, were pulled by two mules.

Apparently the residents liked and supported the service and demanded more. Mule power was replaced by a small steam engine, more tracks were laid, and Denison had what old-timers fondly called

Mule cars like this one provided Denison's first transit system.
— *Drawing from Ralph Douglas Collection*

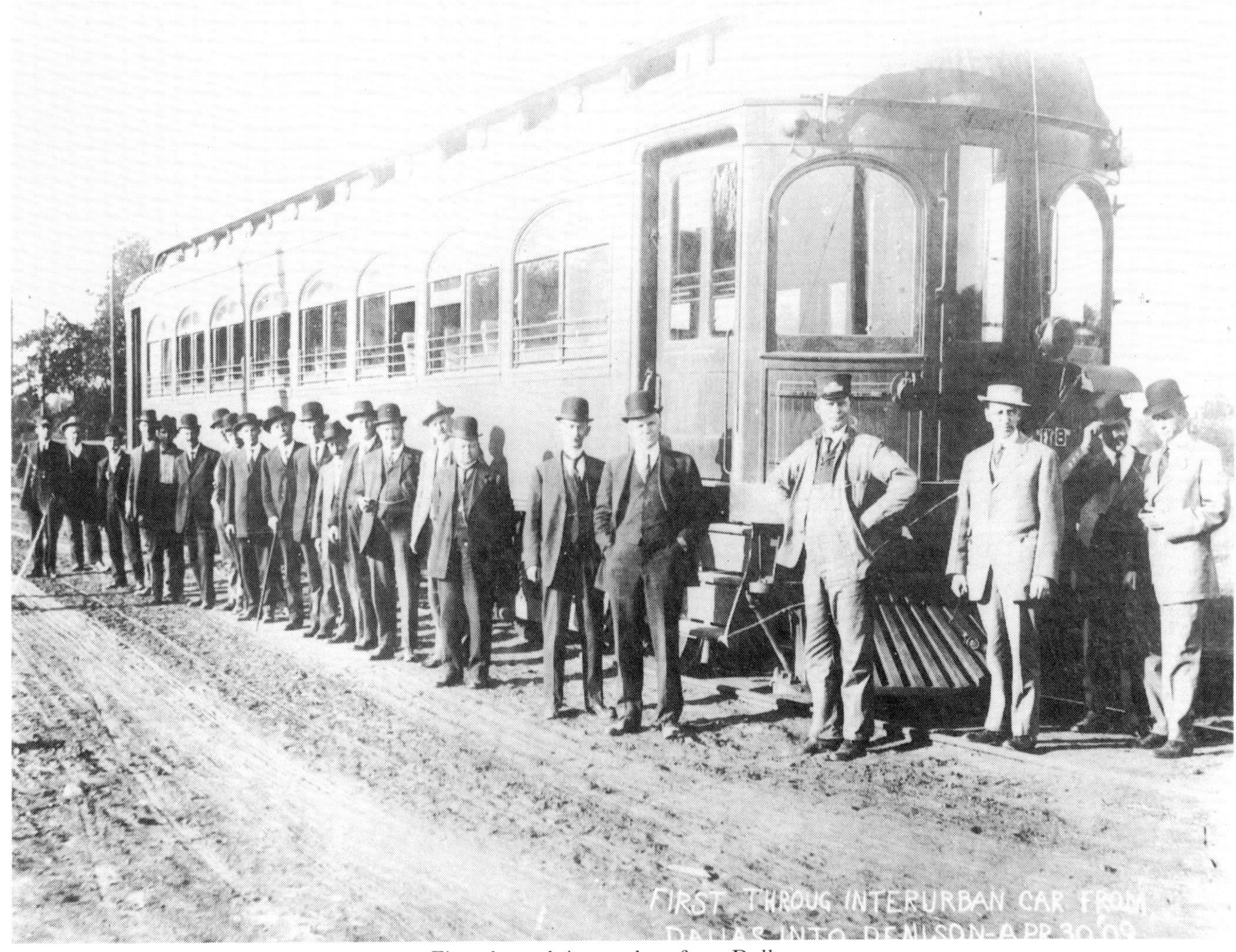

First through interurban from Dallas.

"the dummy line."

It started on Austin Avenue at Woodard Street, continued south over the old wooden viaduct to Coffin Street, then the outskirts of the town limits. At Coffin it turned west to what was then known as College Avenue and went by the old Exposition Hall to Woodlawn. It followed Woodlawn north, then angled to the northwest around the pump station at Waterloo Lake and finally back to Main Street via Scullin Avenue. Within a few years, the little donkey steam engine was replaced by electric street cars and Denison had its first real trolley. More expansion was to come.

From Main Street, the electric line was extended south on Mirick Avenue to Hull Street. There it turned east and ended in the 200 block of East Hull. This took passengers within a block of the old City Hospital, for years the city's major medical facility.

The branch serving north Denison continued west on Main to Scullin, turned north in front of Waples Memorial Methodist Church to Sears Street, then west on Sears to Maurice Avenue just south of Morton Street.

The Interurban Comes to Texas via Denison

In 1896, J. P. Crear, a pioneer in public transit, took over the street railway and had even bigger ideas for the future. He dreamed of extending the electric railway line 10.5 miles to Sherman. Within three years, City Engineer R. L. McWilley had surveyed the route and construction began. On May 1, 1901, the first interurban ever to operate in Texas made its run from Denison to Sherman and back. It was an occasion more festive than the arrival of the first Katy train. Bands played, speeches were made predicting the great future that awaited

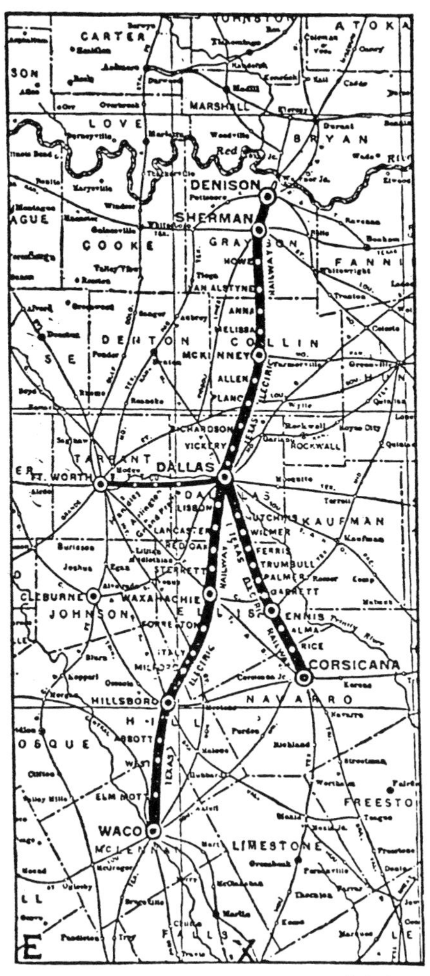

Map of Texas' largest interurban system which began in Denison.
— *Author's Collection*

the twin cities, and the crowd marveled at the progress the new century had brought.

The line was the beginning of a new transportation era. Within a few years, the tracks that had joined Denison and Sherman stretched more than 1,100 miles into the heart of Texas. For almost half a century, the interurban would be a popular travel vehicle for Denison residents. The electric cars sped along at sixty miles an hour with little noise and no pollution. Fares were cheap. A one-way ticket to Dallas was $1.50. A quarter took a passenger from downtown Denison to downtown Sherman in thirty minutes. Cars left Denison every hour from 6:00 A.M. to midnight and returned from Dallas on a similar hourly schedule.

Interurban travel became so popular that one trolley company persuaded the Katy to electrify the railroad's line between Denton and Dallas. For years, interurbans shared the tracks with some of the Katy's crack passenger trains.

As Texas began building better highways and two cars began appearing in every garage, the interurban began its run to oblivion. By 1948, only two — the one between Denison and Dallas and the one serving Houston and Goose Creek — were still in use. The Texas Electric Railway, which owned the Denison-Dallas service, made its last run December 31 of that year.

Denison, where interurbans in Texas were born, may have them again someday. In a world fast running out of the oil that made possible its love affair with the automobile, the interurban may be the rejected suitor that will have another chance. The electric cars were safe (fatal accidents were a rarity), speedy and somewhat luxurious. Best of all, they were relatively quiet, energy efficient and took one from the heart of one city to another without the frustration of freeway traffic.

Whether they return or not, one thing is certain: Without them — and without the railroads — life can never be the same again.

9

When the Army Took Over the Town

"Armies, though always the supporters and tools of absolute power for the time being, are always its destroyers, too."

— Philip Chesterfield (1694–1773)

September 23, 1922, should have been a day of celebration in Denison, but it wasn't. Instead of observing the town's birthday, forty leading citizens gathered at the Chamber of Commerce to telegraph a protest to Governor Pat M. Neff.

For two months, Denison had been an armed camp. Almost 500 soldiers of the Texas National Guard patrolled its streets. Now the governor wanted to send half of the military home — and the town leaders were protesting his decision! They wanted the town to remain under martial law.

In early summer, neither Governor Neff nor the citizens of Denison had foreseen this unusual development in local history. In May and June, plans had been discussed for a huge party to be staged on the upcoming golden jubilee of the town's beginning. That was before a strike had been called on the nation's railroads and more than 1,400 employees in Denison had joined in the walkout. Plans for the gala were shelved.

A railroad strike was nothing new. In 1886, a labor dispute had shut down railroads across the nation, and operations on the Katy and other lines had come to a standstill. There had been riots and strife in some parts of the country, but not in Denison. None was anticipated in the 1922 tie-up, either.

Violence flared, however, early on. The strike began July 1, and on July 11, a group of forty-seven workers arrived aboard a Katy train to replace the shop employees who had walked out. While railroad guards watched helplessly, strikers seized some fifteen of the "scabs" and drove them in cars across the Red River. There they were beaten, put out on the roadside and warned never to return to Denison.

This precipitated a series of cunning high-level plots and intrigues more appropriate to a detective novel than a labor dispute. Before it ended, the Denison situation would involve the president of the United States and ranking U.S. Army officers. It would endanger a major political campaign. It would convert a quiet railroad town into something reminiscent of a prison camp without bars. And it would cause the governor of Texas to slip into Denison in the middle of the night disguised as a job-seeker (a "scab" in the parlance of the strikers).

From the start, politics was a major consideration. The strike caught Governor Neff in the midst of a campaign for reelection. While the railroad managements pressured him to declare martial law, the citizens of Denison — at least, at the beginning of the strike — opposed such action. Since the workers far outnumbered the railroad "brass," Neff stayed with the desires of the majority.

He did not anticipate the entrance of the federal government into what the governor regarded as a matter of state concern. Two days after the incident of the beatings of the unwelcome newcomers by the strikers, however, Secretary of War John W. Weeks warned that if the state didn't act to prevent violence in the strike, he would. The U.S. had 36,000 troops along the Mexican border, and Weeks said he would not hesitate to use them against the striking workers if necessary.

One Strike, Three Rangers

Governor Neff's only response was to send the famous Captain Tom Hickman of the Texas Rangers and two of his men to Denison. Adjutant General Thomas D. Barton, commander of the Texas

The coat of arms of the Denison family, which traces its U.S. ancestry to eleven years after the arrival of the *Mayflower*. The closed helmet denotes an "esquire," or gentleman, and the cutlass in the crest probably refers to military or naval service. The motto *Domus Grata* translates literally as "hospitable house." By implication, it means "beloved home," as the city of Denison surely is.

— *Courtesy of Dr. James Denison Briggs*

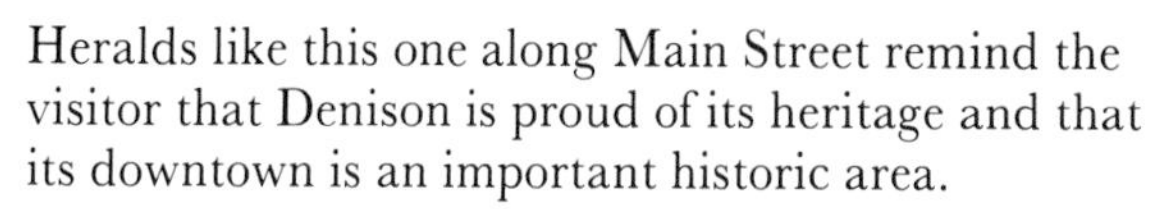

Heralds like this one along Main Street remind the visitor that Denison is proud of its heritage and that its downtown is an important historic area.
— *Photo by Ann Roddy Maguire*

Author Jack Maguire poses under the logo of Denison's flag. The flag was adopted by the first City Council in 1872. In 1946, Maguire discovered a description of the standard while researching in the Fort Worth Public Library. However, it was not officially adopted until 1968.
— *Photo by Ann Roddy Maguire*

A bird's eye view of Denison.

October 17, 1968, was a special day in local history when the unique Main Street project was formally dedicated. Here Mayor Joe Gay, Miss Mickey Mitchusson ("Miss Denison Downtown") and David Bayless, Sr., who spearheaded the pace-setting renovation, prepare to cut the ribbons opening the "new" shopping mall.

— Photo courtesy David Bayless, Sr.

Two views of Main Street after four blocks were converted into a shopping mall. The street itself became a serpentine adorned with trees, shrubbery and rest areas. Strategically placed loud speakers sent music throughout the area and convenient telephones and benches could be found all along the street.

— Photo courtesy David Bayless, Sr.

n the beginning, crowds thronged the new Main treet to shop in the park-like surroundings. As me went on, however, customers found the uburban malls more convenient and the street vas changed again to look much as it did in earlier ears.

— Photo courtesy of David Bayless, Sr.

Although the serpentine curves and much of the shrubbery has disappeared, Main Street still wears a fresh look that is bringing back shops and shoppers once again.

— Photo courtesy David Bayless, Sr.

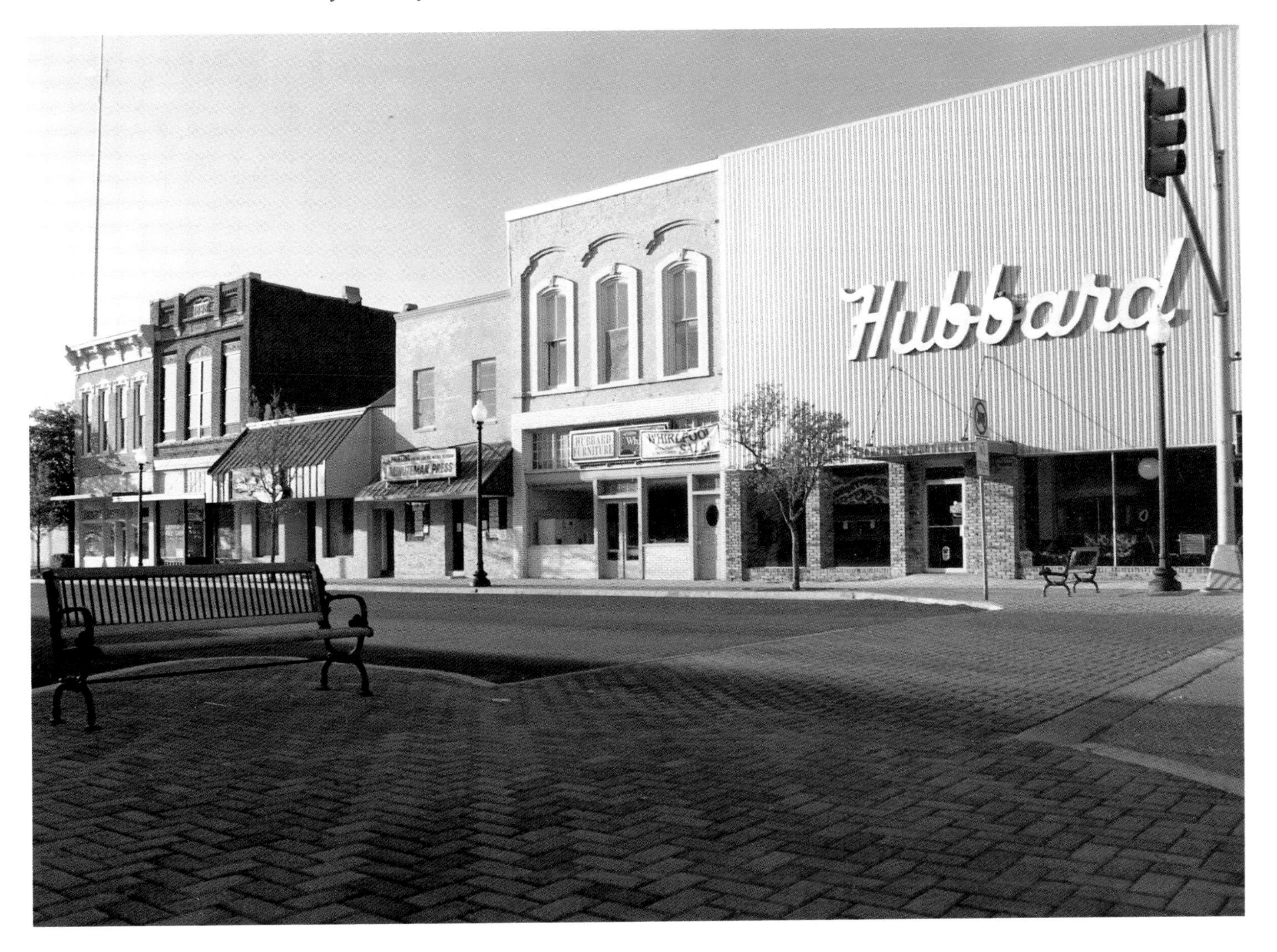

Buses like this one may someday carry shoppers and tourists along the 1950 vintage thoroughfare which Louis Pollaro believes that Denison's historic Main Street can become in the future. He would add trolley cars, theaters showing old movies and shops of the kind that served downtown a half century ago.

— Photo courtesy Pollaro Productions

This house at 1524 West Crawford is believed to be one of the oldest residences still standing in Denison. Records indicate that the property was purchased by S. A. Kilgore shortly after Denison was founded. He opened a brick kiln and built his living quarters on the site. In 1890, when he erected the present home, he incorporated the original structure. It was occupied for several decades by the C. L. Horn family and now is the residence of Mrs. Pete Mannery.

— Photo by Ann Roddy Maguire

Police cars from the 1950s would be used to patrol the "theme street" planners believe can revitalize downtown and make it a tourist attraction. These cars, and the bus in the photo at top, belong to Louis Pollaro. He and his brother operate Pollaro Productions, headquartered on Main. The company produces television commercials for national concerns and shoots scenes locally that become backgrounds for major motion pictures.

— Photo courtesy Pollaro Productions

Union Station, where as many as eighteen passenger trains once stopped each twenty-four hours, is becoming a downtown civic center and tourist attraction. It houses a restaurant, a railroad museum, a television station and offices. The main waiting room is used for receptions and a variety of gala events. C. J. McManus, longtime local merchant and civic leader, purchased the building after it was threatened with destruction.

— Photo courtesy of C. J. McManus

Peggy Roberson of Pottsboro poses in front of the huge mural she painted of the Katy's famed *Texas Special,* one of several she has done to add a festive air to Denison's historic Main Street.

— Photo courtesy of C. J. McManus

U.S. Highway 75, a principal artery between Texas and Oklahoma, intersects Main Street at this point. The Peggy Roberson mural and Union Station, at left, remind tourists that Denison is still "Katy's baby."

— Photo by Ann Roddy Maguire

The eternal flame that marks the grave of President John F. Kennedy in Washington's Arlington Cemetery was designed, built and installed by Col. Clayton B. Lyle of Denison and his crew of U.S. Army Engineers in less than thirty-six hours after it was requested by Mrs. Kennedy. (See Lyle's story in Chapter VII, "They Left Their Mark.")

— Loan of photograph from U.S. Department of Interior arranged through Congressman Lamar Smith of San Antonio

This scene of a Katy train passing in front of the birthplace of Dwight D. Eisenhower at 208 West Day Street was repeated many times daily until the death of that railroad in 1988. The father of the future general of the army and president of the U.S. was a Katy engine wiper when Ike was born in this house October 14, 1890.

— Photo from MKT Archives

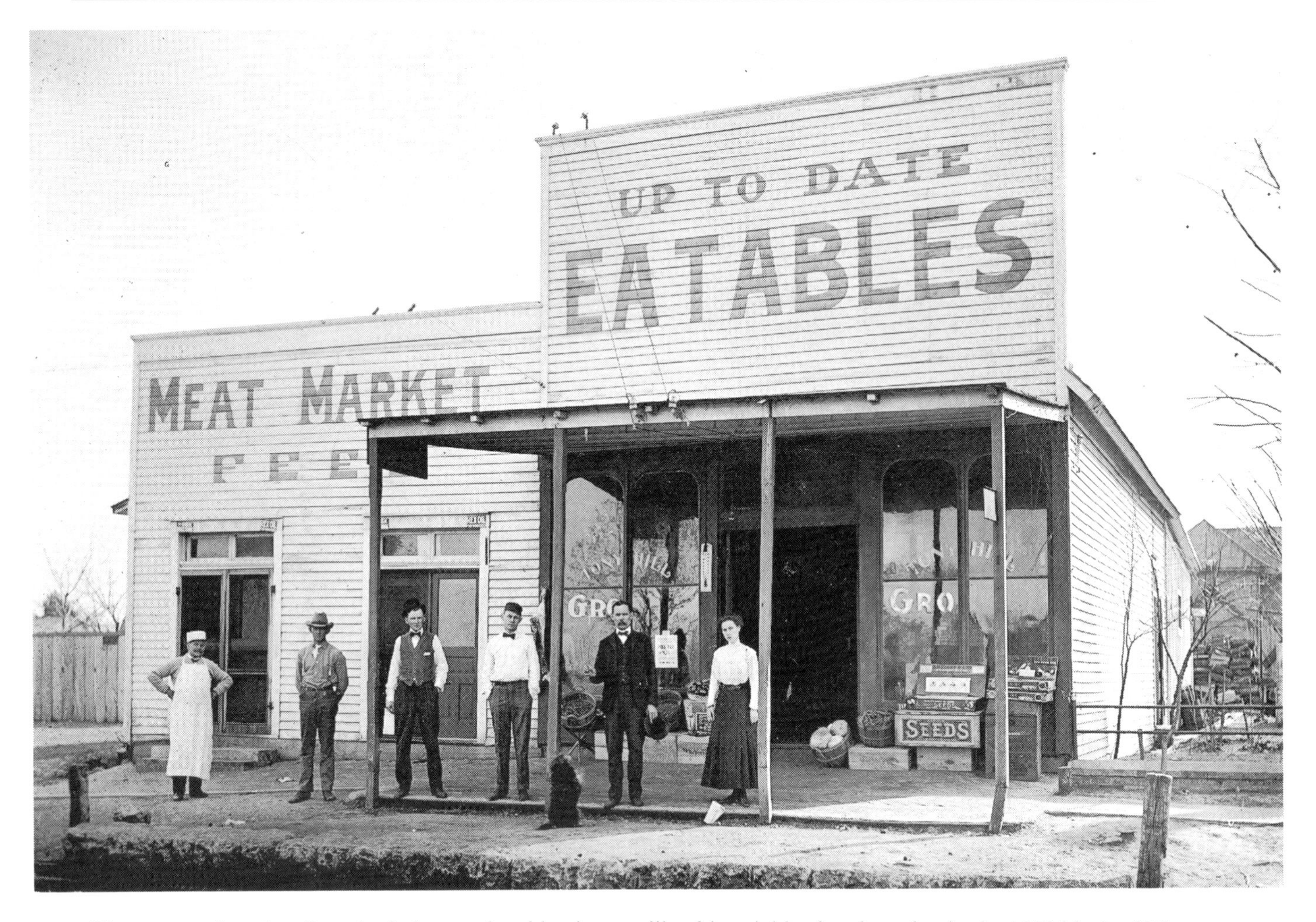

The great railroad strike crippled many local businesses like this neighborhood market in the 1200 block of West Gandy. This was the Tony Hill Grocery, so named because it was in the "toniest" (wealthiest) part of town. A Mr. Frederick, the butcher, is at far left. The next two are not identified. The youngest in the bow tie is H. Coley Hubbard, who later operated his own grocery and then established Hubbard Furniture. At his right is Jesse Whitehurst, the store owner, and Miss Mae Murphy.

— Photo courtesy of Peggy Vaughan

National Guard, came with them. After investigating the situation, they telegraphed Neff that it was "not thought wise to order out troops."

But the matter had reached the White House. President Warren G. Harding was a Republican who had been a newspaper publisher in Ohio. He had a reputation for favoring the interests of big business and was a friend of the railroad tycoons. And he had little love for Governor Neff, a Democrat. The president ordered Colonel Charles S. Lincoln, assistant chief of staff of the Army 8th Corps Area at San Antonio's Fort Sam Houston, to do a special investigation of the events in Denison.

Meanwhile some local civic leaders were sharing President Harding's concern about possible violence. Mayor W. F. Weaver wired Governor Neff, asking for more Rangers. This inspired Neff to undertake a cloak-and-dagger mission of his own. Traveling incognito and heavily disguised, he slipped into Denison aboard a Katy train on the night of July 18. He wanted a one-on-one visit with some of the strikers.

It was between 11:00 P.M. and 1:00 A.M. when the governor, accompanied only by Randolph Bryant, then Grayson County district attorney, began approaching strikers on picket duty in various parts of town. He posed as a new arrival hoping to get work in the shops. Writing years later in his memoirs, Neff said that the answer was always the same: "None of you 'scabs' need apply."

Here Comes the Army

Nevertheless the visit convinced Neff that troops weren't needed in Denison. Instead he announced that more Texas Rangers would be sent. But his decision not to use the National Guard angered the secretary of war. Through Colonel Lincoln, Weeks issued an ultimatum to the governor. In effect, it told Neff that if he didn't call out his troops, a thousand Federal soldiers would be dispatched to Denison immediately.

The governor was furious. A staunch believer in state's rights, he resented interference from Washington. Under the circumstances, however, he felt that he had no choice but to accept what was equivalent to an order from President Harding.

"I was unwilling for Federal troops to march on Texas soil for the purpose of enforcing Texas laws," he wrote later in his memoirs. "I felt that Texas men, and, if need be, Texas bullets and Texas blood, should protect Texas life and property. I took my stand for the supremacy and for the sovereignty of the State."

Thus he reluctantly sent the Texas National Guard to Denison. To house them, a facility was hurriedly erected in Forrest Park. It was named Camp Ellis for Captain J. G. Ellis, Jr., who was killed in France in World War I. During the three months of martial law, the camp was home to up to 536 guardsmen.

The five-story Security Building was the tallest building in Denison's history but even taller ones were being planned until the railroad strike devastated the economy. Later the fifth floor was removed for safety reasons, but the rest of the building survived well over half a century.

— *Denison Herald*

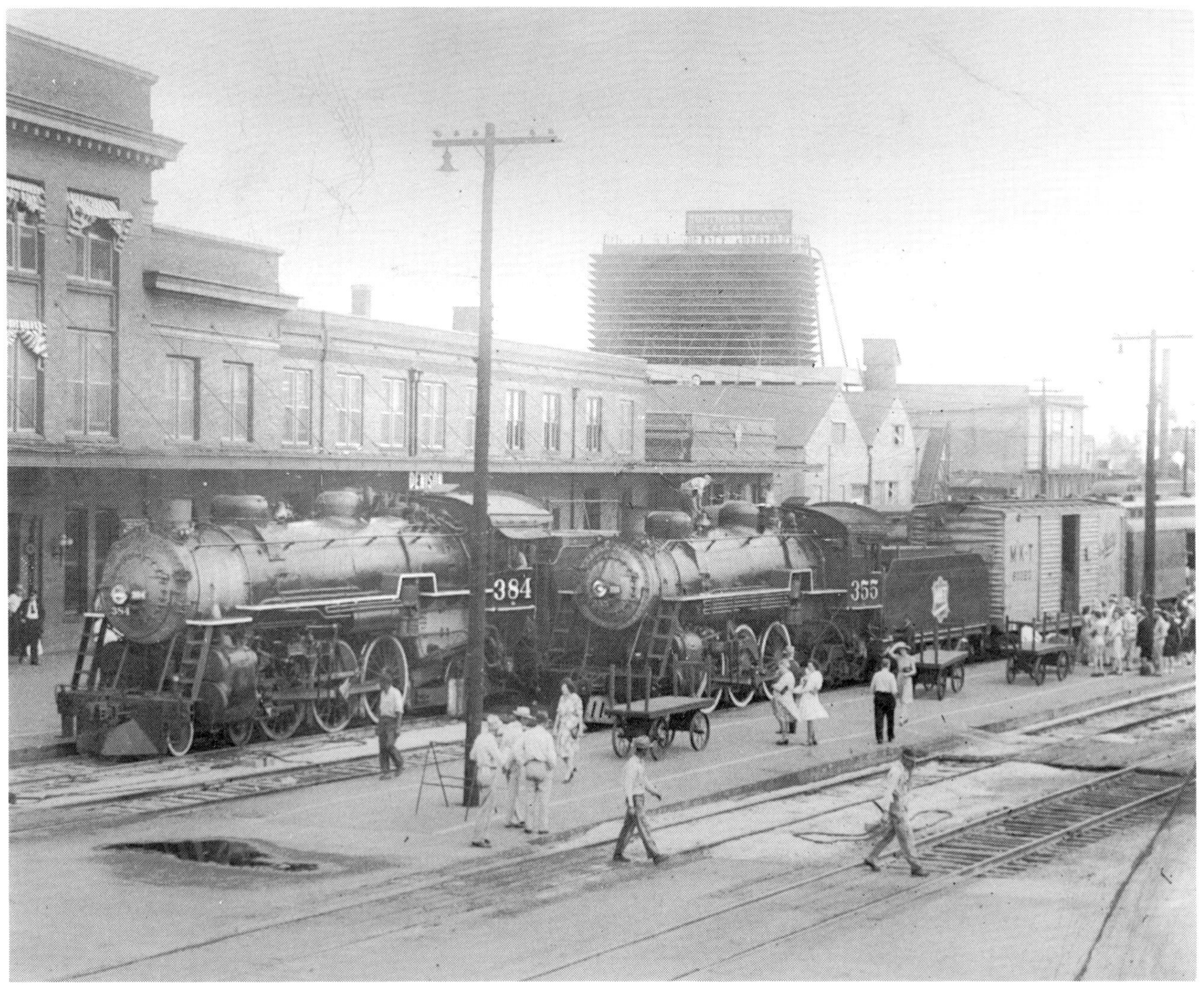

In the early 1940s, the Dallas and Fort Worth sections of the *Texas Special* prepare to leave Union Station on a summer morning.

— *Photo by Claud Easterly*

With the military present, there were a few incidents, but not many. One night somebody cut the electric power lines to the shops. On several occasions, minor damage was done to various pieces of railroad equipment. Pickets tossed rocks at the soldiers a few times, but no one was injured. There were occasional beatings of "scabs" by strikers. And despite the curfews and round-the-clock surveillance by the military, the townspeople and the guardsmen got along well.

The assignment of the 3rd Battalion, 142nd Infantry, was to prevent violence connected with the strike, but in some cases, the troops caused resentment by assuming duties normally reserved for civil authorities. For example, they made almost 300 civilian arrests ranging from serious felonies to minor infractions. They mediated family arguments. In one case, a husband was jailed for deserting his wife.

The Army Decides to Run the Town

The troops went even further. They had been in place less than a month when the commanding officer decided the town was vice-ridden and started "cleaning up" places that sold liquor illegally and where prostitutes still plied their trade. Then shortly before martial law was lifted, the guardsmen were ordered to inspect "all food shops, confectioneries, bakeries and barbers" to make sure they met local sanitation laws. While these actions may have been needed, many objected strenuously

The Simpson Palace Hotel was a Main Street landmark for many years. When Hotel Denison was built behind it on Chestnut Street, the Palace continued to serve as an annex for the new hotel.

— Photo by Claud Easterly

to having the military impose the rules as to how local businesses should operate.

Nevertheless, the same residents who had asked the governor not to send the military in the first place sent the telegram asking him to reconsider his decision to lift martial law. However, by October the strike had weakened. There was never a clear settlement, although the Katy and the other railroads made new agreements with some of the unions. Over the period of the walk-out, some of the strikers had returned to work, but they were considered by many as "scabs." The strike caused hardship and tension among friends and families that would last for years.

On October 21, 1922, Governor Neff issued the formal order sending the guards home and returning Denison's affairs to its civil government. Thus ended the only period in its history when Denison was ruled by the military.

When the National Guard troops departed, the town felt that the "war" had ended. The strike was over and the railroad union members had returned to work. But as is often the case, neither side had won.

By the time the workers in the Katy's locomotive shops had reported back, their jobs weren't there. The Katy had moved the entire operation 206 miles south to Waco. The effect on Denison's economy was dramatic. The population dropped from a pre-strike high of some 17,000 to 13,500. Although the railroad car shops continued to operate, as did one of its largest freight classification yards, the Katy's role in Denison gradually started a downward slide that would continue for decades.

After the 1922 strike, the Katy saw both the quantity and quality of its service decline. Its passenger train fleet, once among the nation's best, began to disappear after World War II. Its *Texas Special,* the premier passenger train in the Southwest when it began operating in 1915 between St. Louis and San Antonio, was the last to go. The train's final run in July 1965 ended all passenger service.

The *coup de grace* to Denison came on May 15, 1988, when the sale of the Katy to the Union Pacific was approved by the Interstate Commerce Commission. With the sale went the jobs of more than 600 Katy employees in the Denison headquarters. Its huge Ray Yards were closed. Other facilities were simply abandoned.

Katy's baby now is Katy's orphan.

10

Refinement on Railroad Avenue

"The great law of culture is: Let each become all that he is capable of being."
— Thomas Carlisle (1775–1881) on *Richter*

Railroad towns, for the most part, are not remembered as cultural oases. Early on, Denison was no exception. Fascinating though trains were, and are, operating them, especially in the days of cinders and steam, was hard and dirty work. Hours were long and employees had little time for events designed to improve the mind or soothe the soul.

The recreational tastes of the citizens of Katy's town were laid bare in a census taken by the *Weekly News* six months after the first lots were sold. It showed that saloons (twenty of them) and houses of prostitution (ten) dominated the business community. However, it also indicated that at least some minds were being stimulated toward loftier goals.

For example, it reported that the first opera house — Dilworth's — had raised its curtain in February. Of even greater importance was the word that a temporary public school had opened on February 6, 1873. Its exact location is not known. City Hall records show that no support came from town funds or other tax money and it was likely that students paid a small tuition. Although it wasn't free, it was open to all and was a move toward a system of education. It had been in session only thirteen days when Professor H. W. Pickett, who had something of a national reputation for his penmanship, started the town's first private school.

The schools and the opera house were the first faltering steps toward the creation of a broad cultural foundation that has persisted for almost 120 years.

The establishment of an educational system was not an easy task. Had the taxpayers been asked to vote bonds for the first school, the measure would have been defeated if one can believe the newspapers of the era. Fortunately the city fathers didn't have to depend on the electorate. There was a provision in the city charter that enabled them to issue up to $50,000 worth of bonds without asking the voters to approve.

School or Jail? Which Shall be First?

The town leaders decided that the two things Denison needed most were a larger school and a jail. The latter also would serve as the city hall. They approved the issuance of up to $20,000 in bonds for the school and $10,000 for the combination prison and municipal headquarters.

A jail of sorts already was in use. It was a cage on wheels, very much like the type used to house wild animals in circus parades. Some of the structures were the height of a two-story building with space to sleep fifteen prisoners on each of the two floors. One such prison which has survived for decades was smaller with only one floor. It is on display at the Grayson County Frontier Village Museum.

Primarily, these contraptions were used to haul prisoners to work on streets and roads. "Road gangs" were a common sight in Texas for many years.

Denison's leadership, however, wanted a jail in a building that could be guarded and that offered more humane quarters for prisoners. It was the school, however, to which they first directed their attention.

They wanted the school to be the first of its kind in the state. It would be tuition-free, of course. Free schools had existed from the beginning of the Republic of Texas. However, the tradition was to teach all students in a group without segregation by

Denison's first jail lacked amenities like bathrooms and TVs, which federal regulations today require, but it served its purpose.

— *Frontier Village Museum*

age or level of achievement. The Denison Educational Institute, as the school would be called, was to offer classes at seven levels based on the students' scholastic progress. This made it unique in all of Texas.

In a town with the reputation of Denison for crime and rowdiness, many citizens thought a good jail should have priority. However, the school project took wing immediately when Robert S. Stevens and his Denison Town Company announced a gift of $1,000 in cash and a block of building lots on West Sears Street for the site. This inspired others to follow suit. Virtually every realtor began offering free land if the school were built in their addition. The site finally chosen was the 700 block of West Main.

This caused controversy. Many objected to the site as being "too far from town." Then Charles Wheelock was chosen as the architect and a civil rebellion almost erupted. Wheelock was a prominent resident of the hated Sherman! On this issue, however, there was no choice. Denison had no architect.

Selling Education with Whiskey

Public education might have been stalled at this point except for the dedication of the city council and the vociferous support of a saloon-keeper.

He was Justin Raynal, and his name would loom large in the history of Denison schools. A native of France, he had arrived in Denison about the time the decision was made to build the Educa-

This obelisk in the Woodard Street parkway across from the old Denison High School honors a saloon-keeper. He was Justin Raynal, who used his money and influence to push education in Denison.

— Photo by Claud Easterly

tional Institute. He opened a bar at the corner of Main and Austin and it soon became a popular gathering place for the town's leading business and professional people.

Raynal had no political clout at the time (later he did serve two terms on the city council). However, he was a vocal enthusiast on the subject of free public education. The stool behind his bar became the platform from which he urged every customer to support the building of the school. Raynal was persuasive. Slowly the community was won over to the side of education.

(When Raynal died, he left his sizeable estate as an endowment to the school system. The town expressed its appreciation by naming a grade school for him. An obelisk bearing nothing but the name "Raynal" stands in the parkway on Woodard Street on the north side of the site where the original Educational Institute was built. It is one of the few statues anywhere honoring a bartender!)

Thanks to Raynal and others, the arguments against the school subsided. Construction began. There were some labor problems, but these were settled with little delay. Although the building was not complete, the Educational Institute opened on March 11, 1874. On the following October 12, it began its first full ten-month term with 291 students.

Although history credits the Educational Institute as the first free graded public school in Texas, the word "free" is a kind of misnomer. This and other public schools did receive some funds from the State of Texas. Incorporated towns, however, were prohibited by law from collecting taxes to operate educational institutions. Thus public schools were supported largely by donations from the citizens.

It was not until March 15, 1875, that the state finally permitted cities to operate and maintain their public schools and to levy a local tax for their support.

Old Schools Don't Die; They Become Ruins

The original site selected for the Educational Institute continued to serve the community for ninety-one years. The name of the school was soon changed to Washington. In 1914, the first building was razed and the beautiful new Denison High School was located on the spacious site. In 1953, a new high school was built on the south edge of the city and the building on Main Street became the B. McDaniel Middle School. In 1963, the middle school also was moved away from downtown.

Since then, the old high school building has stood vacant and neglected, a Main Street eyesore,

This plaque on the east side of the deteriorating old Denison High School building marks the site of the first free graded public school in Texas.

— Photo by Claud Easterly

The Educational Institute was the first free graded public school in Texas. It was built on West Main where the derelict old Denison High School now stands unused and unloved.

— *Frontier Village Museum*

and hearbreak to those who loved it. A plaque on its east wall, however, still proudly proclaims that here, on the site of this ruin, once stood the first free graded public school in Texas.

From 1873 until 1900, it seemed for a while that the number of schools in Denison, both public and private, might grow to equal or even exceed the census of drinking places and dance halls. This did not happen, but these institutions of learning did make significant contributions toward a better life in Denison.

In 1876, the Sisters of St. Mary of Namur founded what would become St. Xavier's Academy, a boarding and day school for girls. In 1883, they established St. Patrick's Parochial School for boys. The two were consolidated in 1924. St. Xavier's closed in 1968 and the building has since been razed.

Denison's first school for blacks was operating two years before St. Xavier's opened. A free school for blacks had opened in January 1874. By March 16, it had grown to a point that it was moved to a church building. It was not until 1886, however, that the first city-supported school for black students was opened.

In addition to St. Xavier's, there was a proliferation of private schools in Katy's town over the next three decades. German settlers, as they did in most Texas communities where they settled, started their own school. Another private school, the Denison Academy, opened in Dodson's Hall at 100 West Main. It was followed by the Gate City Seminary on West Gandy, which offered all grades.

Before the turn of the century, Denison had an-

Denison Commercial College.
— *Denison Herald*

other educational institution that deserves mention. It was more properly known as the Gate City Literary and Commercial Academy, but it is remembered as Professor G. L. Harshaw's Academy. He was the old school educator who built it at 900 West Main, ran it with an iron hand and taught many of those who would become prominent in local businesses and professions.

The Denison Collegiate and Normal Institute had a twenty-five-acre campus southwest of the city, according to an 1887–1890 city directory. By 1893, Kyger's National Commercial College for young men and ladies was operating at Main and Fannin.

The most ambitious of all was the Denison Commercial College. It billed itself as "the largest business college in America" with 86,000 square feet of floor space and the capacity for 1,500 students. Four of Denison's most prominent residents were the officers: T. V. Munson was president,

Professor G. L. Harshaw operated what oldsters still remember as one of the outstanding business "colleges" in Texas.

The Denison Public Library is rated among the best small city libraries in the U.S. It was built on the site of the original home of W. B. Munson, Sr., and incorporates part of the original house in the present building.
— *Photo by Claud Easterly*

Samuel Hanna was vice-president, A. H. Coffin was treasurer and T. W. Roach was secretary.

Libraries Aren't Born — They're Made

Education can't succeed without books, and Denison had a public library a month before it opened its free graded school. Early on the growing business community had established a Board of Trade. And on February 1, 1874, that organization made its first contribution to local culture by opening a library. Its exact location has been lost to history, but it probably was on Main Street. It included files of recent newspapers, a number of books and a supply of pens and stationery.

Like the public schools, it was not entirely free. Users paid a monthly fee of fifty cents. This was not enough to support the operation and it soon closed.

Denison was without a library until 1890, when two culturally-minded young women, Edith Menefee and Cora Lingo, called a meeting of nine of their friends at the home of Mrs. Paul Waples. They voted to organize the XXI Club and Library (so named because the membership would always be limited to twenty-one). Its purpose was to sponsor the "pursuit of study as a means of intellectual culture and general improvement" among its members while also serving the community in myriad ways. It was the second woman's club in Texas; the first, the Bronte Club, was organized in Victoria in 1873.

The organization struggled to survive until J. T. Munson took an interest. He assisted the ladies in incorporating in 1892, making the XXI the second oldest federated women's club in the state. In 1896, he presented them with a deed to two lots fronting on Gandy and extending sixty feet along Scullin. With the property deed went his check for $4,000 to help establish the library. This became the first women's club in Texas to have its own building.

When other communities derisively pointed to

Denison's first Rod and Gun Club building on Randell Lake was a three-story beauty that offered overnight accommodations to members.

— Photo courtesy of Peggy Vaughan

Denison as being the largest town in Texas without a public library, the residents only smiled. The XXI Club collection included more than 3,000 reference books, thousands of other volumes and many rare first editions. By any standards, it ranked in quality alongside most public libraries in cities of similar size.

In 1925, subsoil conditions forced the XXI Club to abandon its two-story home that housed the library. With no adequate place for the books, the members voted to divide them between libraries at the city's two high schools and Austin College.

Another women's group, the Junior Delphi Club, took on the task in 1934 of establishing a public library. It staged a drive for both books and money, and by 1935, it had a home. Miss Eloise Munson loaned the organization the old family home at 300 West Gandy with the only proviso being that the Delphians keep it in repair. It officially opened on November 22 of that year.

In 1948, a special $100,000 bond issue was approved by voters and a new building constructed, keeping the original Munson home as a part of the structure. In 1965, an addition that almost doubled its book capacity was added. That same year, it was named one of the ten best small city libraries in the U.S. by the Book-of-the-Month Club National Library Awards Committee. It has long been ranked among Texas' best small public libraries.

Having established schools and a library, the cultural and social life of early Denison advanced rapidly, largely through a proliferation of lodges, fraternal orders and clubs.

The Country Club That Was

Those who hunted and fished felt the need for a country club and they organized one — in Creed, Colorado!

Members preferred hunting and fishing to golf and the Rocky Mountains offered both in abundance. Nobody objected to the distance from Denison. Rail service was excellent and the usual stay was two weeks.

It was the forerunner of today's Rod and Gun Club, which was established on the northern out-

Women dressed in style in early Denison as this drawing illustrates.

— Drawing by H. D. Morgan

skirts of town. Today it has an outstanding eighteen-hole golf course and offers amenities expected in a successful private club.

Golf had become a popular sport in the 1920's, but it was considered a rich man's game. Many Katy employees, although they knew they would enjoy this popular diversion, couldn't afford it. They solved the problem by building a nine-hole course of their own with the railroad's help.

The Katy Golf Course was located on West Crawford Street on property that had once been a part of the railroad's old Ray Yards. It had sand greens — the members couldn't afford anything better — and players carried mallet-like tools to smooth out the sand in their path before and after putting. W. H. Hall, superintendent of the Katy's telegraph department, and Herman Krattiger, chief of the railroad's telegraph department, spearheaded the move to build the course.

In 1945, the course got its club house — two Katy box cars. And after World War II, it finally got around to putting in grass greens.

Long before golf arrived in Denison, however, a variety of fraternal organizations were formed. The town was less than five months old when the International Order of Odd Fellows established a lodge on February 17, 1873. The preceding January, Dr. Julian C. Feild, the town's leading physician, and B. C. Murray, publisher of the *Daily News,* had started a petition that led to the chartering of the first Masonic lodge on June 6, 1874. Soon came the Benevolent and Protective Order of Elks, the Woodmen of the World, the Knights of Pythias and many others.

Those of a particular ethnic heritage had their own social groups. Denison's large German contingent formed a Turnverin Society in June 1873. It was this organization that introduced to the virile community a dance known as the German — a movement consisting of intricate figures that are improvised and intermingled with waltzes. It was a dance that mesmerized the members of the Sons of Erin, the Irish society, because it was so different from their raucous clog.

Many of these new citizens whose homeland was Europe, and even Asia, were working men. Denison began as a town primarily populated by laborers, and it was inevitable that unions would soon be organized. One of the first was Carpenter's Union Local No. 371, founded in 1888. About the same time, the railroad brotherhoods were rapidly gaining strength and Denison became the home of as many as a dozen lodges representing virtually every craft in that industry.

In addition to protecting the rights of their members, the unions provided a welcome social outlet. Most — particularly the railroad brotherhoods — had ladies' auxiliaries. They sponsored dances, banquets, picnics and other activities designed to bring the members' families closer together in their leisure time.

Still other organizations drew their members from the general public. One was the Denison Philosophical and Social Club, a kind of debating society. Headed by T. V. Munson, the eminent viticulturist, the purpose of this group was to argue the pros and cons of almost any question presented at a meeting. When they weren't debating, they often went to the countryside to hear Munson lecture on the classification, structure and habits of the plants. Also, there were many active card clubs (poker wasn't the only game in town).

Say It With Music

While almost every citizen belonged to one particular group or another, they came together in a body for musical events. Even in the early days of the town, there were occasional impromptu concerts in Forrest Park, the eight beautiful acres near the city's heart which had been donated by J. K. Miller, one of the town's first settlers. Over the ensuing years, the park became a kind of center for home-grown musical entertainment.

Friday night concerts in the park by Ferdinand Dittler and the Municipal Band were popular before World War II. For those with more classical tastes, there was the Philharmonic group of the Verein Vorwarts, another German society. It was succeeded in later years by the Little Symphony Orchestra under the baton of Mrs. Bebe Bodamer. Until the 1940s, railroad employees had their own Katy Band and the Katy Drum and Bugle Corps. Both of these organizations traveled in their own railroad car throughout the surrounding area to appear in parades and festivals.

The First Lady Rotarian

One of the most unique contributions to the culture of the town has been made by Miss Thelma

Braun, daughter of pioneers and long active in many local organizations. For more than sixty years, Miss Braun has been the pianist at weekly meetings of the Denison Rotary Club. Since none of the other 21,000-plus Rotary Clubs around the world can claim such a record for their pianists, Rotary International broke its own rules several years ago to make her an honorary Rotarian.

Today Rotary accepts women as members. But Miss Braun was the first woman in the world to achieve the honor — all in appreciation for her life-long effort to bring a little culture and entertainment to a men's service organization in the town of her birth.

Thelma Braun's name is but one on a long honor roll of both men and women who have contributed to the intellectual and cultural growth of the city. The culture has changed radically over the last century and a quarter as has the physical geography of the original townsite. Life in Denison, however, is still good. Indeed, yes.

This group called itself the Philharmonic and was popular entertainment at Sunday afternoon musicals in Denison homes.

— Photo courtesy of Peggy Vaughan

11

Eisenhower, et al. — Presidents and Denison

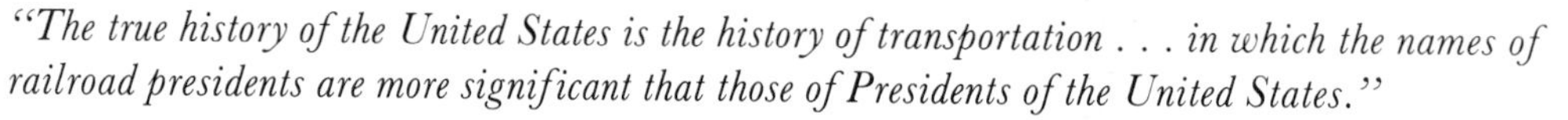

"The true history of the United States is the history of transportation . . . in which the names of railroad presidents are more significant that those of Presidents of the United States."
— Philip Guedalla in *The Hundred Years*

Robert S. Stevens, the general manager of the Katy, was the most important name in America to the prospective buyers who gathered in Denison on September 23, 1872, to bid on the first lots sold in the townsite.

The crowd was aware that Ulysses S. Grant, the general whose armies had defeated those of the South in the recent war, was into his second term as president of the United States. However, if anybody thought of Grant at all that day, it was with hatred because the wounds of the civil conflict had not healed.

On the other hand, Stevens was not only liked and respected as an individual, but he was the operating head of the railroad that had brought the Katy into Texas. And now his Town Company was establishing a community that was destined to become a transportation center. Stevens, and the succession of Katy presidents who followed him over the next century, would indeed be more significant locally than most of those who occupied the White House.

But not all. One — the thirty-fourth president of the U.S. — would be born there. His successor, although he had no connection with Denison except as a one-time visitor, would have a unique and famous memorial created by a Denisonian over his grave in Arlington National Cemetery in Washington. And the thirty-sixth president, the second Texan to hold the office, would be in Denison several times before he would occupy the White House. Three other presidents would visit — and one would "steal" a luxurious Katy lounge car for his special train.

Almost from its beginning, Denison had a connection with the presidency — starting with a relative of the first occupant of that office.

"Washington Slept Here"

This is a slogan Denison could use in its efforts to attract tourists. However, the Washington who slept — indeed, lived — in Katy's town was not George. It was his great nephew.

Dr. Lawrence Augustine Washington moved to Denison in 1874 to practice medicine. His father was the son of Samuel Washington, younger brother of the first president.

Lawrence graduated from medical school in Philadelphia and moved to Texas with his wife, Martha, in 1845. They settled at Vox Populi, a village near Columbus, where he established a medical practice and bought a large farm. He was successful both as a physician and cattle-raiser. Like many others, however, he lost his fortune in the Civil War.

To try and recoup, the Washingtons drove their cattle to Kansas, sold them and remained there until moving to Denison. Once again he started a successful medical practice. Contemporary newspaper accounts indicate that the Washingtons were well-known and well-liked in the community, but little is known of their lives after their return to Texas.

Dr. Washington died August 20, 1882; Martha in July 1891. Both are buried in Denison's Oakwood Cemetery. In July 1991 the National Society of Colonial Dames XVII Century held a ceremony at the gravesite and erected a marker there.

Boos for One President; Welcome for Another

Dr. Washington had been in Denison only a few months when a president of the United States visited for the first time. He was the hated Grant. It

Partly because a Denison High School student needed his help in getting a job, President Franklin D. Roosevelt came to Denison on June 13, 1936.

— *Denison Herald photo*

is not known whether or not the great nephew of the first president met the eighteenth occupant of that office.

It is known that Grant's twelve-hour stay, in what was then a rabidly Democratic town, went almost unnoticed by the press and the populace alike. The Denison *Daily News* gave only four short paragraphs to the stopover of the presidential train on October 23, 1874. And despite Denison's reputation as a tough and even dangerous place, the only guard accompanying the president and his party on a one-hour carriage tour of the town was Lee Hall, the famed deputy sheriff. Hall brought them through without incident.

Grant's party might have had an even less cordial welcome if Stevens, the Katy's general manager, had not been aboard the train. His presence was offset, however, by the fact that also traveling with Grant was General Phil Sheridan. He had made himself especially obnoxious in Texas with his famous statement:

"If I owned both Texas and Hell, I'd rent out Texas and live in Hell!"

Those who missed seeing Grant would have to wait thirty-one years before another president came to visit. This time it was the popular Theodore Roosevelt, but his train paused at the station only a few minutes on April 5, 1905. Much to the chagrin of Denisonians, T. R. was on his way to Sherman! Perhaps the most cruel blow of all to residents of Katy's town, most of whom worked for that railroad, was the fact that the president's train traveled over the competing Houston & Texas Central to Dallas.

The President Who Helped a Denisonian Win a Bet

It was a sense of humor and a willingness to help a youngster win a wager that brought Franklin Delano Roosevelt to Denison on June 13, 1936.

The author of this book was then a sixteen-year-old Denison High School junior with ambitions to be a newspaper reporter. When I applied for a summer job at the Denison *Herald*, however, I was turned down. In that Depression year, dozens of experienced reporters were looking for jobs. The paper had neither the time nor the inclination to train an inexperienced kid.

The graves of Lawrence and Martha Washington in Oakwood Cemetery.
— *Photo by Claud Easterly*

However, Harmon C. Shelby, the paper's wire editor, also had a sense of humor. So when I bet him that I could turn up a story so important it would have to run on page one, Shelby set the terms. If I succeeded, I'd be hired at $5 a week. If I failed, I would never bother the editor again.

I knew that President Roosevelt was going to Dallas to open the Texas Centennial. Since presidential travel in those days was always by train, it was certain that he would have to enter and leave the state through either Texarkana or Denison. A telephone call to J. H. Little, Katy superintendent of transportation, confirmed that the president would leave Texas via Denison.

Next went a formal invitation to President Roosevelt signed by more than 1,000 students at Denison High School. I wrote another, as a cover letter, in which I explained that his train would pause in Denison for twenty minutes to change crews and if he would make a rear platform speech, I'd win my bet and get the job. I also wrote my congressman, Sam Rayburn, and asked him to help get a "yes" from the president.

FDR must have had some sporting blood, because he did accept the invitation. Some 25,000 people — more than the population of Denison at the time — stood in a broiling noonday June sun to greet him. And yes, I got the job.

The President Who Didn't Know Where He was Born

Another occupant of the White House visited Denison on several occasions before he even thought of entering politics, and twice after he left the presidency. But he was world famous before he learned that Katy's town was his birthplace.

He was Dwight David Eisenhower, and he always had a soft spot in his heart for Texas. As a young lieutenant just out of West Point, he was stationed at San Antonio's Fort Sam Houston in 1916. There he met and married a beautiful young visitor from Denver, Colorado, named Mamie Doud. Their first child was born in San Antonio.

In researching the material for this book, the author discovered another startling fact that perhaps neither Ike nor Mamie ever knew. *She also had an indirect connection with Denison.*

According to the official genealogy of the family, Mamie Doud Eisenhower was a descendant of the Denison family!

Eisenhower's assignment in San Antonio was the beginning of his meteroic rise to general of the armies. During these years, he was in and out of Texas, usually traveling on the Katy's *Texas Special.* Like most passengers, it's likely that Eisenhower took the opportunity to stretch his legs on the broad Union Station platform during the train's stop for a

General Eisenhower had never seen his birthplace until June 22, 1945, when four Denisonians drove to Abilene, Kansas, to present a photograph of the house to him. Denison Mayor W. L. Ashburn, far right, hands the picture to the general. At Eisenhower's left is Jack Maguire, author of this book and then a *Herald* reporter, and Fred Conn, *Herald* publisher. The late K. J. Mills, who accompanied the Denison group, is not in the picture.

crew change. If so, however, nobody identified the distinguished officer.

Neither was he aware that the deteriorating white frame house the train passed a few blocks south of Union Station was the place where he was born on October 14, 1890, the son of an engine wiper for the Katy. In fact, long after the name Eisenhower was known all over the world, his official biography listed his birthplace as being Tyler in East Texas. This may have resulted from the fact that the Eisenhowers moved from Denison to Tyler for a brief time before returning to their original home in Abilene, Kansas.

In 1942, when a general named Eisenhower was made commander in chief of the Allied forces in Africa, the media began digging more deeply into his background. The Fort Worth *Star-Telegram* got a tip that Ike's birthplace really was Denison. Sure enough, records at the Tone Abstract Co. verified the fact that in 1890 a family named David J. Eisenhower did live in a house at the northeastern corner of Lamar and Day, but not for long. (The current telephone directory lists the address as 208 West Day.) As soon as the father accumulated enough money, they returned (via Tyler) to Abilene, the cattle town where Ike was to grow up.

This development caused Miss Jennie Jackson, a long-time Denison school teacher, to recall that

General of the Army Dwight D. Eisenhower, born in Denison, October 14, 1890, the first Texan to occupy the nation's highest office.

Only the death of a great leader like Speaker Sam Rayburn of the U.S. Congress (and Denison's congressman) could bring the president of the United States, a future president, and two former occupants of the White House through Denison. President John F. Kennedy, Vice-President Lyndon Johnson, Denison native and former President Dwight D. Eisenhower and former President Harry S. Truman are pictured at the funeral of Rayburn in Bonham in 1961.
— *Courtesy of H. C. Dulaney, Sam Rayburn Library*

she had once rocked an Eisenhower baby when a family of that name was her neighbor. She wrote the general's mother. Mrs. Eisenhower confirmed that Ike was born in Denison.

Although the senior Eisenhower had been an engine wiper, it was Division 177 of the Brotherhood of Locomotive Engineers that started a movement to buy and preserve the general's birthplace as a shrine. When negotiations for the purchase of the house stalled, Fred Conn, publisher of the *Herald*, and E. J. Lilley, a prominent business leader, personally put up the funds.

In 1945, General Eisenhower, now a world hero, came home from Europe to visit his mother and relatives in Abilene. Mayor W. L. Ashburn, Fred Conn, Kenneth Mills, and the author of this book drove to Kansas to greet him, present him a photograph of the birthplace he had never seen and invite him to visit it. Eventually he would make three trips to Denison to see his first home. He came for his initial visit on April 20, 1946, and again during his presidential campaign in 1952.

General Eisenhower retired from the army, became the Republican candidate for president and served two terms — from January 20, 1953, to January 20, 1961. In both elections, Denison, the town to which he had brought so much publicity and honor and which bore the name of his wife's ancestral family, failed to support his bid for the nation's highest office.

Apparently his failure to carry the votes in his birthplace didn't dim his affection for the town. His last visit to the home he really never knew was on September 1, 1965. He died in 1969.

An Eternal Flame for a Fallen President

John Fitzgerald Kennedy, the thirty-fifth president of the United States, never paid an official visit to Denison.

In fact, the only time he ever saw Denison was in November 1961, when the young president flew into Perrin Field on a sad mission. He was en route to the funeral of a great Texan, Sam Rayburn, in Bonham. That city had no airport that could accommodate *Air Force One,* so the presidential party landed at Perrin Air Force Base. After the service, Kennedy flew back to Washington and probably never gave Denison another thought. Almost exactly two years later to the day, on a political trip to Dallas, he was assassinated — a tragedy that would involve a former Denisonian.

He was Colonel Clayton B. Lyle, Jr. Born in Greenville, he moved to Denison as a child, graduated from Denison High School in 1931, took an engineering degree at Texas A&M and went on to a fascinating career that included the building of a unique memorial to the fallen President Kennedy.

It was to the Corps of Army Engineers, and Lyle, that Jacqueline Kennedy turned for the design and construction of the flame device that would burn eternally on the grave of the late president in Washington's Arlington National Cemetery.

On November 24, 1963, two days after President Kennedy's assassination, Colonel Lyle had returned to his home in Washington from an assignment in Europe. He chose to remain at home and avoid the bedlam which had engulfed the capital. Like most of his countrymen, he was watching television coverage of the tragedy at Dallas when his telephone rang. Calling was Lt. Gen. Walter K. Wilson, Jr., chief of U.S. Army Engineers.

"We've got a problem," his boss told him. "We have to have an eternal flame for the president's grave by eight o'clock tomorrow morning. You've got the job. Now get with it."

The request had come from the First Lady. According to *Death of a President,* William Manchester's account of the assassination, it happened this way.

Mrs. Kennedy, along with the new president and Mrs. Johnson, had accompanied her husband's body to the Capitol rotunda that same Sunday morning. It was to lie in state there until the following day when the state funeral was scheduled.

Col. Clayton B. Lyle of Denison was asked by Mrs. Kennedy to design and build the eternal flame memorial that marks the grave of the late president in Washington's Arlington Cemetery.

— Department of the Army Photo

Somehow, Mrs. Kennedy told Manchester, the idea for an eternal flame "just came into my head." She had seen such a flame at the memorial to unknown soldiers at the Arc de Triomphe in Paris and wanted a similar salute to the slain president.

Although Colonel Lyle had never before had such an assignment, he went to work at once.

"I just thought up the idea and made a few sketches," he recalls.

During Lyle's twenty-seven years of military service as an army engineer, building missile sites in West Germany and airport runways in South Korea had been among his assignments. In 1956, he had led a Task Force to Canada to construct the International Geophysical Year Rocket Program — a $25 million project. A technical job like putting together a lamp, a pipe and two gas cannisters was not a major engineering project.

There was no time to design and build such a

device from scratch. He and his staff scrounged Washington electric shops and found a luau lamp — the kind commonly used to illuminate patio parties. They tested it by pouring water on it, blasting it with air and trying every way they could devise to douse the flame. It continued to burn.

At nearby Fort Belvoir, Virginia, a crew of officers and enlisted men made a base for the lamp. Next they welded metal strips into a frame to support it. Their colleagues at Fort Myers, which adjoins Arlington National Cemetery, bought containers of propane gas, hooked them to a one-inch line and buried the line in the hillside above the president's grave. The job was completed within thirty hours.

The makeshift device worked perfectly. However, in March 1965, when the Kennedy grave was relocated to a permanent site in Arlington, the lamp was replaced and hooked to an underground gas line so that the propane canisters no longer had to be used.

"I got more publicity out of the eternal flame than from all of the other projects, major and minor, that I accomplished in a lifetime," Lyle said. "It was an honor to be a part of it, but I'd rather not have had to do it."

How Denison Helped LBJ

As a boy growing up in the Texas Hill Country, Lyndon Baines Johnson knew intuitively that some day he was going to make a bid for the presidency of the United States. His intuition also taught him that the best way to succeed in politics is to get the support of the power structure. And he learned that this can be accomplished in myriad ways — including traveling on a train at the right moment with the right people.

That's how Denison — and the Katy Railroad — helped boost him toward the White House.

In 1937, Johnson was elected to Congress from the 10th District of Texas. His home at the time was Austin, the city where his father, a member of the Texas Legislature, had known another young House member named Sam Rayburn from Bonham. After serving in Texas, Rayburn had been elected to Congress in 1906 and now held the second highest position in the House of Representatives — that of majority leader. The young congressman from Texas set out to develop a close relationship with "Mr. Sam."

His effort became even more intense in 1940 when Rayburn was elected Speaker of the House — a position regarded by some as second only to the presidency in importance and prestige. Johnson began to devise unobstrusive ways to spend as much time as possible with his mentor and friend. One excellent way, when the opportunity arose, was to ride with the Speaker as he traveled between Bonham and Washington on the Katy's *Texas Special*.

The author vividly recalls one such incident in the summer of 1940, when a tall figure wearing a white ten-gallon Stetson walked into the editorial offices of the Denison *Herald* about 4:00 P.M. one afternoon.

"My name is Lyndon Johnson," he said, "and I want to buy somebody a cup of coffee."

No one else was in the office at the time, so we walked down to Carl's Cafe and had coffee. It was a visit that would develop into a friendship that lasted until LBJ's death. But that's another story.

Over the coffee, he said that he knew Speaker Rayburn would be arriving in Denison to board the train to Washington and that he had made reservations in the same Pullman car. Johnson listed a long agenda that he intended to discuss with him. As it turned out, however, Mr. Rayburn had a last-minute change in plans and had to cancel his trip and Johnson decided he needed to get to Dallas and catch a plane to Austin.

He asked me to drive him, but I didn't have a car. I telephoned my boss, *Herald* publisher Fred Conn, at home and explained. Although it was then 7:00 P.M., Fred drove the future president of the United States to Love Field, returning home well after midnight.

LBJ missed that particular opportunity to ride the train with Rayburn from Denison to Washington, but there were others. Rayburn did not like flying, although Johnson preferred the speed of airplanes. Nevertheless, he never hesitated to take the train if he knew that Rayburn would be aboard, and if his own schedule permitted the relaxed trip of two nights and a day.

The President Who Commandeered a Katy Lounge

Harry Truman, the thirty-third president of the United States, never paid an official visit to

Not many editors of small city newspapers get a chance to walk and talk with the president of the United States, but here Claud Easterly of the *Herald* accompanies Harry S. Truman on a stroll down Denison's Main Street.

Denison. However, in 1961, he did join Eisenhower, Kennedy, and Johnson at the funeral of Speaker Rayburn in Bonham, and the trip brought him through Denison. That visit also provided an unforgettable experience for the two previous occupants of the White House and the one who would assume the office two years later. It happened this way:

En route from Perrin Field, located between Denison and Sherman, to the Rayburn funeral, the limousines stopped at Bales' lumber yard on the outskirts of Bonham. The occupants walked over to a corral where Bales kept a small herd of goats.

The animals took one look at the distinguished visitors and the entire herd promptly collapsed on their backs in a trance, their feet quivering in the air! They remained in this position until Dwight D. Eisenhower, Harry S. Truman and Lyndon B. Johnson returned to their cars and sped off to the rites for the Speaker of the House.

Flattering as it may have seemed to the distinguished visitors, it wasn't the presence of two past and one future president of the United States that put the goats into their tizzy. The Bonham animals were a unique breed that falls into a frozen trance at any unexpected sight, sound or movement. The hosts of the famous guests felt that the diversion of the fainting goats would help lighten the burden of their sad mission, and it did.

On one of his stops in Denison, Mr. Truman took time for his favorite exercise, walking, and was accompanied by Claud Easterly, then editor of the *Denison Herald.*

The ex-president and Easterly reminisced about many things as they walked, but no mention was made of the time when Truman "borrowed" a Katy Railroad lounge car, without permission, on one of his trips to Texas during his campaign for re-election to the presidency in 1948.

Truman was the last presidential candidate to use a special train extensively for whistle-stop appearances all across the land. When the president traveled by train, he had his own private railway car — an elaborate hotel-on-wheels. Bullet-proof windows had been installed and enough extra steel had been added under the car to resist almost any explosion short of an atomic bomb.

This car, known as the *Ferdinand Magellan,* was the rolling White House when the president was aboard. It included a kitchen, master bedroom, two smaller bedrooms, quarters for the chef and butler, a dining room that seated twelve and a sitting room. There also was a rear platform equipped with microphones and loud speakers for use when the president made his "whistle stop" speeches.

Except for the *Magellan* and a baggage car equipped as a state-of-the-art communications center, the rest of the train was standard railroad equipment. White House staff, the press corps, Secret Service agents and any others traveling with the president were quartered in regular sleeping cars furnished by the Pullman Company. However, the dining and lounge cars were provided by the host railroad while the train was traveling on that line. When POTUS (code name for the train) was switched onto another railroad, these two cars were taken off and those of the new host railroad added.

This was a system that had worked well until 1948, when Harry Truman took his campaign to the people via the high iron. The White House transportation office chose the Katy for a large segment of the trip through Texas. The Katy had been famous for years for the superb meals it served on its diners. Its full-length lounge cars with their bars and luxurious appointments were the envy of competing railroads and the delight of travelers. Thus it's not surprising that when President Truman ventured from his private car to visit in the Katy lounge, he decided that this car belonged in his train's permanent consist.

It did not concern the president that this was contrary to railroad policy. When POTUS left the Katy's line for another railroad, he ordered that the lounge car stay on the train. He kept it for several more days of campaigning through the West before the Katy managed to retrieve it and put it back into regular service on the famed *Texas Special.*

After Truman left the White House, anytime he traveled over the Katy he was offered the use of the private car of one of the railroad officials. For years, it was the railroad's policy to offer the same courtesy to other former national leaders. John Nance Garner, the first Texan to be vice-president of the U.S., often traveled aboard Katy Business Car 400 or 401 between San Antonio and St. Louis. Speaker Sam Rayburn, who always rode the *Texas Special* on trips between Denison and Washington, usually turned down the Katy's offer of a private car and was content with a lower berth in a regular Pullman.

As mentioned earlier, Lyndon Johnson made

many trips via Katy from his home in Austin to and from Washington, and knew the Union Station platform well from his walks during the Denison stop. However, by 1960, when he became vice-president and then moved on to the White House, *Air Force One* had replaced POTUS as the choice for presidential travel.

Today when a president flies to Texas, he doesn't even get a glimpse of Denison from 35,000 feet. *Air Force One*'s routing from Washington usually brings its distinguished passenger into Texas in the area of Texarkana.

12

To Your Good Health

"Medicine has been defined as the art or science of amusing a sick man with frivolous speculations about his disorder, and of tampering ingeniously till nature either kills or cures him."
— Lord Francis Jeffrey (1773–1850)

Life insurance was a commodity not easily available in early Denison. Those pioneers who arrived with the Katy in 1872 suddenly found their policies either not renewed or canceled outright.

The problem lay in the fact that most insurance companies at the time were headquartered in places like New York, Chicago and Hartford. Their underwriters hardly knew Texas; almost none had heard of the infant town the Katy had spawned. However, they had read enough geography to know that the lowlands along the Red River in Louisiana were anything but conducive to good health. The death rate there from malaria, pneumonia, fevers and other maladies was much higher than mortality tables predicted.

Denison was only four miles from that "sickly" Red River, so it was reasonable for these distant experts to assume that the lives of residents in the new town had to be in danger. Since insurance companies profit most when claims are lowest, they responded with wholesale cancelations of policies in the area.

Just as the insurance moguls were ignorant of geography, the citizens of Denison had never heard of something called "public relations." In fact, the term would not even enter the language for another fifty years. Through their elected leaders and the new Board of Trade, however, they set out to educate the insurance industry in simple geography in what certainly must rank among the nation's first calculated efforts to induce a segment of the public to change an opinion.

First, they fired off letters and telegrams to the insurance centers informing them that only seven months after the first lots were sold, Denison had built and was operating a fifty-bed hospital on Skiddy Street. Not even the much older and larger county seat, Sherman, had such a facility. In fact, the Denison City Hospital was the only hospice in all of North Texas.

Secondly, the town had two prominent physicians in residence. Chief of the hospital was Dr. Julian C. Feild. Assisting him was Dr. Alex W. Acheson, a University of Pennsylvania Medical School graduate who had left a lucrative practice in Philadelphia to come to the frontier town as surgeon for the Katy Railroad.

The third effort was to teach the insurance people some geography. The Board of Trade pointed out that if healthful living had been the only consideration in locating Denison, the townsite selected still would have won hands down. Denison was not in the lowlands — its altitude placed it eighty feet above the river. They described the dry, good weather, bragging that even during the winter, "there is seldom ten days . . . that a person cannot be out of doors without, or with, a light wrap."

There was much more of the same. Apparently it convinced the insurers. The companies not only quit canceling policies, but put new agents in the area actively soliciting business.

Despite the town's best efforts to advertise itself as a virtual health resort, serious illness was a problem. A year after its founding, an epidemic of cholera threatened to kill off most of the population.

Was It Cholera or Ptomaine?

Tainted barbecue, eaten at a picnic staged on September 27, 1873, to celebrate the town's first birthday, was blamed. Within ten days, twelve people had died, many others were dangerously ill and almost everyone who had attended developed at least mild symptoms. Whether the disease was cholera or severe stomach poisoning is arguable. Most modern physicians think it was the latter.

Despite the fact that cholera cases were being reported all over the nation at the time, B. C. Murray, the fiery editor of the *Daily News,* believed that the disease had left Denison untouched. He insisted in his paper that the deaths were due to "intemperate living" and from eating food prepared in the filthy kitchens of the many local boarding houses.

It is unknown how many lives the epidemic finally claimed. Reporting of such statistics in 1873 was vague, to say the least. However, one survivor who was still alive in 1964 estimated that the toll might have been more than one hundred.

In an interview published in the *Herald* in July 1964, Mrs. Bill Linden said that "burials were held day and night. Most of those who didn't die moved out, bag and baggage, but slowly filtered back after the epidemic ended."

Within a month most of the ill either had died or recovered. Editor Murray, who never recognized the existence of the epidemic, now led a fight to close the hospital. With the recent health crisis over and the city's treasury low, many Denisonians agreed. On October 28, 1873, the city commission voted to shut the institution's doors and remove Dr. Feild from the town's payroll.

It would be forty years before Denison got another hospital.

Meanwhile, local physicians had cared for the community's health as best they could. The more prosperous opened small clinics where they could treat patients and perform some surgery. Although these facilities provided for the population's most urgent health care needs, there was growing agitation for a community hospital.

Denison had continued its steady growth. By the turn of the century, the railroad center had a population of 15,000, of which an estimated 3,000 were Katy employees. This fact had prompted railroad officials to consider building a hospital for its employees and opening it to the public for a fee. In addition, several doctors had talked about pooling their funds and opening their own general facility.

By 1910, matters had come to a head and there was a demand for a public fund drive to build a hospital. When that effort stalled, Denisonians insisted that the city call an election and issue bonds for the project. The bonds were approved by the electorate, but a fight then developed over the location of

Even in a city that prides itself on the good health of its citizens, deaths do occur. Here is a funeral procession, 1930 vintage, getting ready to start.

— *Jenkins Studio Photo*

the proposed hospital.

One group wanted the facility in the 1300 block of West Main — a site favored by Dr. Acheson, who now was also mayor. He offered to donate two lots for this purpose. Others, however, pushed for a location on East Hull, and this property finally was purchased. However, many citizens objected and asked the city commission to rescind its decision and locate the hospital in an area bounded by Main and Morgan streets and Chandler and Rusk avenues. This proposal was rejected, and construction began at the 411 East Hull Street site on February 12, 1913.

Hospitals Galore

While Denison leaders were trying to decide where to put the city hospital, the Katy had opened a small clinic on the fourth floor of the Security Building to serve its own employees. The city's hope was that its new hospital, when completed, could be leased to the Katy to operate. The railroad rejected that idea, but did agree to use the new City Hospital for emergency surgery. Meanwhile, Drs. J. G. Ellis, Sr., and L. C. Ellis signed a contract to operate the hospital, and it opened under their management on February 11, 1914.

However, the Katy did not discard plans for a facility of its own. To encourage such a project, the city deeded twenty-seven acres in northwest Denison to the Katy Railroad for use as a hospital site. Work started in 1920, and the sixty-five-bed facility was opened on November 1, 1921, with Dr. T. J. Long of Denison as the division surgeon and Dr. A. G. Sneed as the resident physician.

Over the years, several private medical facilities were established. From 1914 until 1919, Dr. Long and Dr. Arthur M. Freels operated a small hospital in the 600 block of West Main. In 1928, while still on the Katy Hospital staff, Drs. Long and Sneed purchased a home in the 400 block of West Woodard and converted it into a clinic. Later they built an addition to the house and opened the two-story, fifteen-bed Long-Sneed Hospital with Dr. E. L. Hailey as one of the medical staff.

Until about 1925, Denison blacks had no hospital of their own. In that year, Dr. Roscoe C. Riddle opened his Mercy Hospital at 1030 West Munson. It restricted its patients to blacks, and they came from as far away as Louisiana. Black men always had been accepted as patients at the Katy Hospital, and blacks of either sex were treated at

Keeping railroads healthy and safe means constant monitoring. Here is one of the types of motor cars used by the Katy to inspect its tracks.

— *Author's Collection*

City Hospital. Mercy closed in the mid-1940's.

A second facility for the black community was the eight-bed, three-nurse Holloway Infirmary. Dr. J. M. Holloway was the only physician, but like Dr. Riddle, he maintained a staff of consultants, including several white doctors.

Once the contract with the Drs. Ellis to manage the City Hospital ended, the management was assumed by all of the physicians practicing there. In 1943, when the old building was in serious need of repairs and a complete modernization, the Sisters of Divine Providence, a Catholic sisterhood that operated extensive hospital properties, offered to take it over. In exchange for a deed to the property from the city, the Sisters agreed to remodel and operate it as a first-rate medical facility to be known as Madonna Hospital.

There was, however, an ordinance that prohibited gifts from the municipality to a charity. Therefore, the Sisters agreed to purchase the property at its appraised value of $4,500 if the funds could be raised locally as a gift. In exchange, the Sisterhood was to spend a minimum of $50,000 on rehabilitating the facility.

As it turned out, $50,000 wasn't enough. To put the hospital in shape, it had to be almost totally rebuilt and the ultimate cost was $176,000. Local banks stepped in to lend a third of the money, another third was raised by public subscription and the Sisters anted up the remaining third. The "new" Madonna opened on September 1, 1945 — a state-of-the-art facility at the time.

What to Do with a Used Hospital?

In this modern age, hospitals are like automobiles. A new car is "used" the moment the buyer drives it away from the dealership. Medical advances also come so quickly that even the newest hospital is outdated almost by the day it opens. This proved true of Madonna. By the mid-1950's, it had become too small to serve the population and again was in serious need of repairs and more modern equipment.

City Hospital on East Hull Street served for years as the medical center for this area.
— *Photo by Claud Easterly*

Memorial Hospital was the beginning of the present Texoma Medical Center. It occupies the site where the Katy Employees' Hospital stood for many years.

— *Photo by Claud Easterly*

Efforts to solve the problem with the Sisters of Divine Providence failed, so a professional hospital consultant was employed. His recommendation was that Denison should build a new facility. The city government already had reached its borrowing limit, however, and could not issue the needed revenue bonds. But a Hospital Authority could, and the Council proceeded to appoint one.

The Authority board of directors had eight members: Robert Baker, Vernon Beckham, J. D. Bond, Fred Conn, Charles Gullett, Sam Harwell, Miss Eloise Munson, Ralph Porter and R. R. Rutherford. Each had a special interest in the project. For example, Porter had been a member of the old hospital board and had just left the office of mayor.

Dr. Alex W. Acheson, one of the first physicians to practice in Katy's town, who later became a civic leader and an advocate of Red River navigation.

Beckham had served in the legislature and had important Austin contacts. Miss Munson and the Munson Foundation had long been supporters of health care, and Fred Conn, the publisher of the Denison *Herald,* had a compelling motivation.

Conn admitted that he always had been "allergic to hospitals." Active in civic affairs, his special concern was industrial development and he had been involved in bringing several new businesses to Denison. Then in the early 1950's, his young son was in Madonna Hospital for emergency surgery. As he waited for the child to go to the operating room, he heard two nuns discussing whether or not some instruments had been sterilized. Neither seemed to know.

Whether this conversation had any bearing on the events that followed is conjecture. But the Conn youngster died shortly after the surgery. It was then that the father vowed to do everything he could to help Denison get a modern hospital.

By 1961, architects had plans drawn for an eighty-bed hospital with sufficient ancillary facilities to sustain a 150-bed operation. They recommended this as only a start. By 1990, they hoped a 300-bed acute care hospital would be in place with the most modern equipment available. The next steps were to get a $900,000 federal grant under the Hill-Burton Hospital Act, issue bonds for $875,000 of the $1.1 million the Hospital Authority was authorized to sell, and proceed with the project.

Location was an immediate problem. Once again, the age-old rivalry with neighboring Sherman reared its head. The county seat city was been proud of its two hospitals — one public and one operated by Catholic nuns — and they had served hundreds of Denison patients over the years. Now Denison was planning what it hoped would be the finest medical facility north of Dallas, and it wanted Sherman patients to have easy access. Waterloo Park on the Loy Lake Road, just off U.S. 75, would put all of Sherman within fifteen minutes of the new hospital.

However, money wasn't available to purchase the land. So when the Katy Employees' Hospital Association offered the city fourteen acres adjacent to the railroad hospital in exchange for ancillary services like laboratories, operating rooms, diet kitchens, etc., the Hospital Authority Board grabbed the offer. An all-weather tunnel, built at Katy expense, would connect the two institutions.

Madonna was one of the many hospitals that served Denison before the Texoma Medical Center was built on the site of the old Katy Employees' Hospital.

Texoma Medical Center today and its staff of specialists serve the health needs of a large section of North Texas and southern Oklahoma.

— *Photo by Claud Easterly*

Later the old Katy Hospital, having long outgrown its usefulness, was razed.

In 1965, the new Memorial Hospital opened as a 144-bed institution. It would grow still further and become the great Texoma Medical Center that it is today, serving not only Denison, but Sherman and many other communities in both Texas and southern Oklahoma.

A principal benefactor in making Texoma a star among medical centers in the Southwest is one whose own stardom in the entertainment world is legendary. She is Reba McEntire, the first lady of country music. Reba grew up in a Katy town — Kiowa, Oklahoma — but the famous singer and actress has adopted Texoma Medical Center as her favorite charity and Denison as her second home.

Her love affair with Denison and its medical center began when the first of her six nieces and nephews was born at TMC. Since then, the other five also have entered the world there. So in 1987, when the hospital was planning its $2.5 million Smith Women's and Children's Center, she agreed to help by giving a concert as a fund-raiser. She has repeated the concerts each year since. The Women's and Children's Center includes state-of-the-art nurseries and a neo-natal intensive care unit. Because of her interest in children, and in appreciation of her generosity, this section of it was named the Reba McEntire Nurseries when the Center was opened in 1989.

This not only delighted Miss McEntire, but inspired still another gift. It is a facility to be called Reba's Ranch House — a home away from home for families with seriously ill patients hospitalized in Texoma Medical Center. In addition to its primary function as a guest house, it will offer meeting facilities for support groups, patient education classes, nutritional and social services and a playground for children.

It's no wonder that when this daughter of an Oklahoma rancher comes to town, a banner goes up on Main Street that reads:

"Welcome, Reba! We love you!"

Reba McEntire, the "first lady of country music," is an Oklahoman who has adopted Denison as a second home. Here she breaks ground for Reba's Ranch House, a "home away from home" she is building to house families of seriously ill patients at Texoma Medical Center.

13

Alleys and Boulevards: Streets of Dreams

"Along the brittle treacherous bright streets of memory comes my heart, singing like an idiot, whispering like a drunken man."

— e. e. cummings (1894–1962)

If Denison's Main Street is its heart, the other streets are its arteries and the alleys its veins that keep the lifeblood flowing. Except that the alley has all but disappeared with the changing times, and it's a pity.

In the original plat of the townsite, alleys were as important as streets. They bisected each block and gave the residents of the streets on either side a depository for their garbage, a rear entrance to their property and, most important of all, provided a passage way for the horse-drawn scavenger wagons that collected the contents of the outdoor toilets that served each home.

Even with the advent of modern plumbing, the alley continued to provide access for garbage trucks on their weekly visit. And for children growing up in the years before World War II, the narrow passageway was a special place. It was a made-to-order playground. Autos rarely used them (except downtown, where trucks found them convenient for deliveries). Every alley provided secret alcoves so vital to games like "Hide and Seek." And after dark, it was a perfect setting for "Piggy Wants a Signal," and a platform for ghost stories.

Treasure in Trash

The alley also was a treasure trove for the industrious. The garbage of childless adult neighbors produced many empty cans that once held Waples-Platter products — containers whose labels, when carefully removed and collected in large numbers, could be traded for prizes like baseball gloves, footballs and a long list of other desirables. More affluent (or, perhaps, unknowing) neighbors sometimes discarded empty soda pop bottles worth a penny each at the neighborhood grocery.

Now, however, Denison's alleys — along with streetcars and interurbans — have all but disappeared. The alley, like the sidewalk, is no longer required in the newer subdivisions. Some of these do have "mini streets" in the rear, but they exist only to provide access to the garages on each block. The real alley is gone.

Except for the wishful nostalgia of those lucky enough to grow up knowing the passages out back, the vanishing of the alley as a vein in the city's circulatory system has not damaged the general health of the community. However, its disappearance is a part of the changing times that have had a traumatic effect on Main Street — the city's heart.

The thoroughfare that stretches in a straight line between the eastern and western town limits was intended by A. H. Coffin and the other planners to be called Main Street for a reason: They saw it as forever being the center of commerce, the medium of local communication, the busy vortex of the everyday life of the community. They knew that people would go to Main Street to shop, to see their physician and lawyer, to bank or just to walk. The street gave the town a sense of community.

Not One, but Three Viaducts

Guiding all traffic, pedestrian and horse-drawn, toward Main Street was a concern of early city leaders. Those living and working north of Morgan had no problem — the town's central district was easily accessible from all directions. For those south of Morgan, however, the situation was different. The roundhouse, shops and switching yards of the Katy Railroad stretched six blocks

In the early 1880s, Main was bustling with businesses and people.
— *Denison Herald*

Main Street moved to Guadalcanal during World War II, when C. J. McManus opened a Dad and Lad's Store to serve his buddies in the CB's.

from Lamar on the East to Mirick on the West. Residents living between the two avenues had to detour to one or the other to get downtown.

The problem was solved in the early 1880's by the building of a wooden viaduct. Primitive by today's standards, it nevertheless carried the tracks of the "dummy line" urban rail system and the first mule-powered streetcar, as well as a walkway for pedestrians.

It served until 1915, when Denison became involved in a controversy over plans for a viaduct to replace the original. This was to be a two-lane concrete bridge that ultimately gave way in 1954 to the present four-lane version. The argument over the 1915 structure arose over its design that allowed it to start on one avenue, then do a dog-leg and veer east to exit on another.

Many citizens argued that politics were behind the strange design, and probably with good reason. E. E. Davis, a member of the City Commission, owned a livery stable at the corner of Chestnut and Rusk. (It later evolved into one of the city's largest automobile dealerships.) Naturally, Mr. Davis urged that the viaduct connect with Rusk Avenue.

The simplest, least expensive design called for a straight bridge that connected with Rusk on the south as well as the north. However, another Commission member and later mayor, F. G. Coleman, owned a grocery store at the corner of Munson Street and Austin Avenue, a block east of Rusk. The new viaduct was built with a sharp curve so that its exits were at Austin and Rusk. Midway in the structure was a steel stairway to allow Katy shop employees who walked to work (and most did) to get to and from their jobs easily.

Denison's third viaduct came thirty-nine years later as part of a renewal project of U.S. Highway 75. Businesses in the Sugar Bottom shopping area on South Armstrong Avenue objected because the old route of the major highway took many cars by their shops each day. The new road would enter the city and cross Main Street on Austin Avenue. For a while, the issue divided the town, but bonds were voted on and the new viaduct was built. It opened to traffic November 26, 1954. A traffic signal at the intersection of Austin and Main guaranteed that at least part of the U.S. 75 traffic would have a brief stop — time to have a glance up the street that still was Denison's heart.

Even then, however, Main Street, like those in most small towns, was showing its age. Although still healthy in 1954, there were signs of decay and obsolescence. The people who had treasured it, and whom it had served so well, had begun to outgrow it. The exodus from downtown was a post-World War II phenomenon that was spreading across the land.

America had become a nation on wheels, its way of life dictated by the automobile. Even decisions on where to shop were based on the availability of easy parking rather than loyalty to a particular business. Denison, which for three-quarters of a century had been a rather compact town geographically, had begun to see suburban developments on its outskirts.

A Sweet Place Called "Sugar Bottom"

In truth, Denison from early times had been one of the very few small towns that had a "suburban" business district. It was a stretch of a few blocks along south Armstrong Avenue and adjoining streets which the townspeople called "Sugar Bottom." Exactly why this small commercial area developed some distance from downtown and how it got its name are facts lost to history. There are two versions, both probably apocryphal, as to how its unusual designation originated.

One story is that a gang of rowdy boys who called themselves the "Huckleberry Gang" became angry with Gideon Stephens, the cantankerous owner of the neighborhood grocery. One night they broke into his store, took a barrel of sugar and dumped it along South Armstrong. From then on, the name "Sugar Bottom" stuck.

The other — and more likely — story is that a Katy crew was switching freight cars where the tracks still cross Armstrong Avenue. The main line had not been cleared when a passenger train rounded the curve and splintered a freight car loaded with sugar. The sweet cargo spilled into the street. At any rate, Sugar Bottom got its distinctive monicker and some little fame. Shanty Morrell, who grew up there and went on to become a well-known orchestra leader in Texas, wrote a ballad called the "Sugar Bottom Blues." It was a mild hit in the state.

The Malady of Main Street

South Armstrong's Sugar Bottom was what today would be called a "strip" center of small shops and offices. It included a couple of grocers, a furniture store, a shoe repair shop, a barber and at least two gasoline stations. With this as a kind of model, similar strips away from downtown began to spring up in the 1950's, at busy intersections where the traffic was heavy but parking plentiful. Main Street merchants, many of whom had been in the same location for decades, were concerned.

Their first response was to "beautify" and "modernize." They began overlaying their great stone and red brick buildings with stucco, blue-mirrored glass and tile in the manner of the old false fronts of the early West. Since such adornments didn't appear to be enough, they added gaudy signs made of thousands of feet of multi-colored neon tubing. The upper floors, left vacant by the doctors and dentists and lawyers who already had deserted downtown for the neighborhoods, either had their windows boarded or covered by the remodeled exterior.

These remedies slowed, but didn't cure, what appeared to be a fatal illness of Main Street. So C. J. McManus decided to try another prescription.

McManus, who had moved to Denison with his family when he was thirteen, had entered business for himself at nineteen. His Dad & Lad's Clothing Stores in Denison, Dallas and other cities (and even on Guadalcanal when he was in World War II), were well known to Texans. Although he had sold his Denison store and moved to Dallas in 1952, he continued to have a special interest in what would always be his home town. He owned many of the deteriorating buildings in the 100 and 200 blocks of West Main, and in 1960, he began refurbishing them. McManus' efforts, laudatory as they were, didn't stop the decline of Main Street, however.

The time had come for more drastic measures.

In 1966, Lynwood Massey, then president of Texas Power & Light Co., and David Bayless, Sr., prominent business and civic leader, learned that Grand Junction, Colorado, had turned three blocks of a principal business street into a downtown mall. The idea had won an All-American City Award and had revitalized the center of the town. Massey and Bayless, certain that Denison had to do something drastic to meet the challenge of the changing times, went to Colorado to see the project first-hand.

Nickel Parking and the "Street of Dreams"

From this beginning grew Denison Downtown, Inc., a non-profit group of interested citizens with Bayless as president. With a tentative budget of over $250,000 and the backing of most of the business community, the group set out to convert the 200, 300 and 400 blocks of Main Street into a shopping park. They tore down ten buildings to start, remodeled others, removed old buildings on Woodard Street to provide parking lots and rear entrances for some Main Street establishments and transformed the three blocks into a "street of dreams."

The wide, straight street itself became a serpentine, with trees, flower beds and live music from speakers concealed along the way. There were benches lining the walks, telephone kiosks, and parking lots that charged only five cents an hour. It was a magnificent undertaking by people who loved the great old street and wanted to keep it the lively, busy place it had been since 1872.

It was the grandest of ideas, but it didn't work. Instead Main Street became a kind of central wasteland. Confused by the serpentine street, motorists skirted the mall. Pedestrians disappeared, as did many businesses. Vacancies, which had been a problem, now became the rule rather than the exception. Even the two large retailers that had stayed through the revitalization left to join the popular malls on Highway 75 between Denison and Sherman.

In 1989, again at the expense of the property owners, the street was changed back from a serpentine to a wide thoroughfare. But still more businesses moved from Main Street to the shopping centers which were accessible by fifty-five-mile-per-hour highways and had free parking that was virtually unlimited.

Denison hasn't given up, however, on trying to save the street everybody seems to love but most ignore. C. J. McManus, seventy-six in 1991 and long retired, is still doing his bit. After the Katy Railroad pulled out of Denison forever, he traded property and cash and bought the Union Station, one of the finest railroad depots in the nation in a town the size of Denison. It is the anchor of Main Street.

How a Railroad Depot Revitalized a Town

The spacious, lofty first floor has become a kind of civic center, a nostalgic setting for everything from large meetings to craft festivals. An excellent restaurant on the mezzanine balcony allows diners to look down on the activities in what once was the busy waiting room where passengers on as many as twenty daily trains disembarked or relaxed

Jerdy Gary, Denison resident and son of a former Oklahoma governor, poses with a gasoline pump used in the city's first auto service station.

— Photo by Claud Easterly

while awaiting the next arrival. Overflow crowds at the various events can spill out onto the ancient brick platform or to the small, but beautiful, park that marks the entrance.

Tourists stop by the station to dine, visit the ever expanding railroad museum housed in what were once Katy offices or just to explore a building of fascination for everyone who remembers the romance of "the high iron." In addition to the railroad museum, a television station and a variety of offices are there. Service clubs like Kiwanis, Lions and Rotary meet for their weekly luncheons at the Depot Restaurant banquet room on the second floor, and other groups come and go.

As a result, Union Station is almost as busy, at least some of the time, as it was in the heyday of the railroads.

McManus didn't stop with saving the railroad depot. He also bought the building behind the station known as the old Peanut Factory. This favorite nut not only is roasted there, but is turned into a variety of products sold nationally by mail and through famous stores like Neiman-Marcus. He also has bought and remodeled or restored almost every building in the 100 block of West Main.

Denison bills itself as "historic" and Main Street is a volume of history in itself. To point this up, and to add a unique splash of color, McManus hired local artist Vicki Roberson to paint murals on several of the buildings he owns. The one tourists like best, and which they often stop to photograph, covers 2,100 square feet on the Austin Avenue side of the former Katy office building which fronts on Main. It is a mural half a block long that depicts the state's most famous, the *Texas Special,* speeding through a field of grain behind No. 396, one of the railroad's fleet of steam locomotives. The original painting by famed artist Howard Fogg was commissioned by the railroad a half century ago and forms the dust jacket for this book.

There are others who believe that Main Street has a future. One is Louis Pollaro who, with his brother, Joe, has gained national attention for Denison with their company that produces motion pictures and television commercials (often using Main Street as a set). He would like to see Main converted into a "theme" street of 1950 vintage. He would uncover the original brick, long paved over, and run streetcars again on the tracks that are still there.

A collector of antique automobiles himself, he would use such cars as downtown taxis and operate a mid-century bus to haul other passengers. To once again "revitalize" the buildings, Pollaro would remove the stucco and neon and present them as they were in the 1950's. In so doing, he believes that at least six blocks west of Union Station could be changed into a street of memories that would attract tourists from all over.

The idea is one almost certain to receive some attention from a new Downtown Denison Association which is in place now. Its mission is to promote, preserve and develop that area. Main Street may get another chance yet.

Roads to Fame

Although Main has been the principal thoroughfare since the townsite was first laid out and likely always will be, most other streets are named for individuals who had roles in the development of the city.

Robert S. Stevens and his colleagues who planned the town originally, however, drew their street names from three sources: Texas heroes, officials of the Katy Railroad and some of the first settlers. For reasons unknown, Stevens did not memorialize himself this way. Strangely enough, however, Mirick Avenue was named for his secretary, H. D. Mirick. (An early public school, now closed, did bear Stevens' name.)

More than fifty years ago, in gathering information for a little book titled *A Short History of Denison, Texas* (1938: The F. W. Miller Co., Denison), the author had long interviews with Alex W. Acheson, one of the town's earliest physicians, and A. H. Coffin, who surveyed the townsite. Each was honored with a street name. From notes made by a high school student during those interviews so long ago come these facts about how other thoroughfares got their names:

Woodard, Morgan, Gandy, Sears, Bond, Walker, Johnson, Eddy and Brown all were either Katy directors or employees. Travis, Crockett, Lamar, Houston, Austin, Rusk and Burnet honor Texas heroes.

Morton is the only Denison street named for a U.S. public official. He was Levi P. Morton, New York banker and politician. Morton was president of the Katy at the time it was building into Denison.

Skiddy Street as it looked in 1873.
— Drawing by Dr. H. D. Morgan

H.D.Morgan
"HERE ON SKIDDY STREET, MILLIE HIPS HELD FORTH WITH HER "SOILED DOVES" FROM SEDALIA - EVERY THIRD BUILDING ... WAS A SALOON."!

Later he became vice-president of the United States under Benjamin Harrison and then was governor of New York.

Scullin Avenue memorializes John Scullin who, except for Robert S. Stevens, may have been the most important Katy official in Denison's history. He was the principal contractor who built almost every mile of the railroad from Fort Scott, Kansas, to the new town in Texas.

One of the few ranking railroad officials who chose Denison as a permanent home was Edward Perry, for whom an avenue was named. He was the Katy's cashier, and stayed on to become vice-president of the State National Bank.

Francis Skiddy is the only Katy official to have the honor rescinded, after having a street named for him. Skiddy, the first street south of Main, quickly degenerated into the local red light district. It was populated mostly by saloons, gambling houses and brothels and became the "sin center" of Denison. So when the area farther west on Skiddy started developing into one of the finer residential districts, these home-owners were embarrassed when asked to give their address. They prevailed on the city commission to change the name to Chestnut after a favorite tree.

Nelson was named for Charles W. Nelson and Shepherd for L. W. Shepherd, both agents for the Denison Town Company. Day honors W. H. Day, the first real estate agent and later a partner of W. B. Munson in a realty company. Heron honors the surveyor who laid out that addition to the town. Although there were three Munson brothers, the street of that name honors W. B., Sr., the first to arrive on the scene.

Murray is a tribute to B. C. Murray, the oft-mentioned editor of the Denison *Daily News* and later the *Gazetteer*. The first mayor of Denison, L. S. Owings, is remembered by the street of that name.

Hanna memorializes Sam Hanna, who helped to establish the Waples Platter Grocery Co. Bullock Street was named for one of the 147 home-seekers brought to Denison from Boston via special train by the Town Company in an attempt to sell them lots (Bullock's first name has been lost to history).

Not every transportation personality for whom a street is named worked for the Katy. The Armstrong who gave his name to that avenue operated a stage line. Local businessmen were honored, too. J. M. Barrett, who moved from Sedalia, Missouri,

When banker Hull absconded with his financial institution's money and caused the first bank failure in Denison's history, there were no photographers around. However, Dr. H. D. Morgan captures the incident in this drawing.

to open a Denison slaughter house, is remembered with an avenue. Chandler honors Bob Chandler, an early furniture dealer. Harrison Tone, clerk of the Town Company, rated an avenue named for him. Maurice Avenue bears the name of C. E. Maurice, first city recorder.

Hull Street has, surprisingly, kept its name, although at one time there were some efforts to change it. William L. Hull, who ran one of the town's earliest restaurants, was also Denison's first banker. All went well until Monday, March 3, 1873, when his Mechanics' Bank failed to open.

Bank failures, as they still do today, happened frequently. It seems, however, that Banker Hull had left town the preceding Saturday night with all of the institution's cash in his luggage. He drove to Sherman with a buggy and team hired from a livery stable. There he hired another rig and traveled on to Weston in Collin County. He sent the driver on to McKinney and disappeared.

Hull proved, however, that he had some compassion for his depositors. When the sheriff opened the bank safe, he found a note asking forgiveness.

The note explained that his hasty departure

was because he had honored a bad draft for $5,850 — a large amount of money for that time. He said that this, plus other debts, had left him no other choice, but that he would see to it, once he solved his own financial problems, that no depositor would lose a dime. These hopes dimmed when an examination of his books indicated that he may have left with between $10,000 and $70,000.

Hull was arrested a few days later, returned to Sherman and jailed. Whether his customers ever were repaid is another of history's unanswered questions. But one thing is certain: After almost twelve decades, an important street in south Denison still bears his name.

14

Good Times in the Old Town

"Care to our coffin adds a nail, no doubt;
And every grin, so merry, draws one out."
—John Wolcott (1733–1819)

An early newspaperman, vintage 1873, delighted in saying that people went to Sherman for religion and to Denison for fun.

That wasn't entirely true. Denison's First Presbyterian Church was organized on December 23, 1872—two days before the first Katy train arrived. By mid-1873, the Episcopalians, Methodists, Baptists and Catholics all had congregations organized and one had built a sanctuary. An interdenominational chapel was open on Woodard Street.

It was true, however, that Denison also had its Skiddy Street with gambling tables, dance halls and brothels. A census taken by the *Daily News* March 13, 1873, was proof positive that houses of amusement outranked religious institutions in numbers if not popularity. It listed twenty saloons, ten brothels (dance halls were included) and only one church actually standing.

All of the entertainment wasn't limited to Skiddy Street, however. On July 4, 1873, Denison celebrated its first observance of American independence with a basket picnic held at Colbert, Cherokee Nation. The Katy ran a special train the six miles to Colbert Station with between 400 and 500 passengers aboard. An estimated 1,200 actually attended and a table more than 100 feet long was required to serve the meal. There were games like pitching horseshoes and washers. Children played dolls and marbles. Adults danced far into the night.

There were cultural pursuits, too. The Dilworth Opera House had opened in February 1873 at Gandy and Austin. Jerry Nolan, who later would also own a livery stable, had a show place on the second floor of 200 West Main where family entertainment was presented. In 1875, J. B. McDougall purchased a place farther west in the same block and opened an elaborate opera house.

Picnics in Forrest Park were a tradition almost from the first arrivals. Aware of what the Boston Common and New York's Central Park contribute to those cities, seven acres near the projected downtown, a gift from J. K. Miller, were set aside for a permanent recreation area. Later a part of it was used to build Munson Stadium, playing field of the Denison High School Yellow Jackets, but most of Forrest Park still remains an attractive park land.

In the 1920's, the Munson family gave another beautiful park to the city. Located just off of U.S. Highway 75 north, it is a popular place for picnics and relaxation. Loy Park, created between Denison and Sherman to honor the late Jake J. Loy, former legislator and long-time Grayson County judge, has been a favorite spot since the 1940's. It got an extra added attraction in 1967 when a Frontier Village and Museum was started on a thirty-acre site inside the park. It is still adding historic structures brought in from around the county.

Rx for Whiskey

Ideally, the Frontier Village Museum at Loy Park should include an authentic saloon from the period, since these drinking emporiums contributed so much to the economic and social atmosphere of the town.

The lives of these "gentlemen's clubs" were relatively short. Their eventual doom was being predicted even as they proliferated on Denison's Skiddy and Main streets. Denison was less than a decade old when the Women's Temperance Union and other groups began a national campaign designed to restore total sobriety to a nation of tipplers. Their goal was not only to close all saloons, but also to ban the manufacture, transportation and sale of all intoxicating liquors.

Favorable sentiment for the proposal slowly built across America, and on December 18, 1917, Congress approved the 18th Amendment to the Constitution. Before it could become effective, it had to be ratified by the legislatures in two-thirds of the states — a matter expected to take seven years. Ratification took only twenty-five months. Only Connecticut and Rhode Island voted against the amendment. After January 16, 1919, no beverage containing alcohol was legally allowed in the country.

This created a lucrative market for bootleggers. Like the rest of the nation Denison had its share of these entrepreneurs, and they continued to supply customers at a price. Much of their product was manufactured from Grayson County corn and produced in crude distilleries hidden in brush along the river. The raw bourbon was known as "white lightning." Liquors such as scotch, gin, rum and vodka were imported by big city operators like Chicago's Al Capone and distributed to local bootleggers around the country.

Some Denisonians, appalled at the high prices of bootlegged stuff, turned to their own resources. The more adventurous discovered how to turn juniper berries into a drink known as "bathtub gin." Wild grapes, persimmons, apricots, peaches and even apples became ingredients for a variety of home-produced alcoholic beverages. Many became relatively expert at brewing potent beer at home.

By 1933, with the nation in the grip of the worst economic depression in its history, the country did an about-face on the subject of drinking. Congress repealed the 18th Amendment, with the states' ratification.

Liquor was legal again, but only within whatever laws the various states would approve. Texas was slow to change. Oklahoma legalized beer, but Texas did not follow suit immediately. Even after Texas legalized beer, there were conflicting laws on other alcoholic beverages. For a while, liquor by the drink was available only in private clubs. Some areas permitted the purchase in package stores; others remained totally "dry."

However, there are always some who can find ways to get around the letter of the law. Traditionally, whiskey had been regarded by some as a "medicine" as well as an intoxicant. Early dentists used it as an anesthesia. It was not unusual for surgeons to do the same thing if no morphine was available to ease the pain of the knife. A long drink of liquor was thought to be an antidote for snakebite venom.

Thus it was not surprising that some enterprising individuals used the supposed medicinal values of alcohol to make it legally available to anyone claiming the need for it as a nostrum for illness. Selling whiskey as a panacea for a variety of illnesses became a profitable sideline for some Denison drug stores.

It worked this way. The pharmacy would install an elderly, long retired physician at a small table by the prescription counter. Prospective customers for liquor first visited the doctor's "office" where, after a question or two, the medic made his diagnosis and prescribed a pint of whiskey as a cure. He wrote out a prescription and collected twenty-five cents for his trouble. The patient then stepped over to the pharmacist, presented the prescription, and purchased the whiskey.

The prescription could not be refilled. If a second pint of spirits seemed necessary, another visit to the physician and a new twenty-five-cent prescription was required.

Distant Denisonians Remember

Perhaps the most unusual picnic has been an annual affair for more than sixty-seven years, and it's staged far from home. It's the gathering of the Denison, Texas, Reunion Association on the second Sunday of each August in Long Beach, California. In 1924, Minnie R. Benner invited a group of fellow former Denisonians to a small picnic at her home in Santa Monica. The reunion has been held each year since, often attracting as many as 300 to 400.

Gone but not forgotten is Woodlake, the forty-acre park between Denison and Sherman which was built in 1901 by the interurban company to promote travel. It was so named because of its heavy woods and beautiful lake, and it was a favorite hideaway from the hustle and bustle of the two growing towns that it served. Fare to the park on the electric cars was a dime from either Denison or Sherman (fifteen cents round trip) and half the fun of the outing was riding the trolleys that sometimes reached speeds of forty miles an hour on a straight stretch.

When Denisonians move to faraway places, they don't forget their home. Here is the crowd of expatriates now living in California who turned out for the annual Denison Society picnic in 1940.

— *Denison Society photo*

Woodlake even boasted a casino, but more accurately it should have been called an auditorium. There was no gambling of any kind. It was more like a community theater, and during the spring and summer vaudeville acts and theatrical companies gave regular performances. It was a favorite of religious groups, too, and for years was the site of the annual Southern Baptist Encampment. Many camped on the grounds for this event, and special interurbans were operated from Denison and Sherman to take others to enjoy the hymn singing and old-time gospel messages.

Cooling Off at Bush's

Swimming was a special delight that Woodlake offered. Except for this resort, aquatic activities were limited to places like the Red River (which could be treacherous for the unwary) and favorite swimming holes that existed in a few area creeks. This was true until a far-sighted citizen named J. O. Bush decided early in the 1900's that Denison needed a permanent swimming hole and gave it one.

Bush's Swimming Pool, located at 1600 West Johnson Street, was a success from the start. That the facilities were primitive by 1990 standards didn't deter the crowds. The 600,000-gallon pool, which varied from one to ten feet in depth, was built on the site of an abandoned rock quarry and opened in 1917. The water was supplied from two nearby wells and was not changed as often as today's laws require — not nearly as often, according to those who remember swimming there. Admission was fifteen cents for those under twelve and twenty-five cents for adults.

It mattered not that most people didn't own bathing suits — those could be rented in the adjoining bath houses which also provided showers and restrooms. Plenty of parking around the 120-foot square pool allowed visitors to sit in their buggies or cars and watch the action in the water.

For more than twenty years, Bush's was a favorite recreation spot. However, the air-conditioning of local movie theaters and the building of Loy Lake took away much of the business and the pool closed on Labor Day, 1939.

When not swimming at Bush's or relaxing at Woodlake, residents had a choice of a variety of other amusements. Before the arrival of radio in the pre-1930's and television more than a decade later, most entertainment was live on stage. This accounted for the early popularity of the opera houses. Even when movie theaters appeared on the scene, live vaudeville acts usually were a part of the program.

In 1906, "The Great Train Robbery," a one-reel thriller, was the first movie ever shown in Denison — a portent of things to come. Nevertheless, a

There was a time when everybody who was anybody went to Woodlake for fun.
— *Chamber of Commerce*

year later, Harrison Tone, the staid abstract expert, and Hiram Brooks bought the building in the 500 block of West Main that later would house the Jennings Furniture Co. and now Barrett Drug. They also opened the Brookstone Opera House.

Moving Pictures Come to Town

Silent motion pictures were becoming the new wave of entertainment, however. Soon theaters like the Arcade, Empire, Princess, Rex, Star and Queen were all drawing crowds in the 200 block of West Main. Apparently this competition had little effect on the Tone and Brooks venture. They opened still another show place, the Brookstone Airdrome, across the street at the corner of Main and Mirick. As the name suggests, the Airdrome was a theater under the stars. It had no roof.

By 1920, when the Rialto was built, Denison had gone big time in the movie business. For a town of fewer than 20,000, the Rialto was the miniscule equivalent of New York's Rockefeller Center. It had cushioned opera-type seats, a stage big enough to accommodate both actors and an orchestra and it even boasted an organ. It also had a balcony — the first in town.

Eventually the Rialto and Star (later renamed the State) were acquired by a chain and the Rio, also in the 200 block of West Main, was built by the same company. Across the street, the Princess, a former vaudeville house, was bought by B. Legg and became the Superba. It remained a locally-owned movie theater into the early 1970's.

In the thirties, forties and into the fifties, a trip to the movies for the younger set was not complete without a stop at either the White Pig or the Tom-Tom Drive-Ins. They stood across from each other — the Tom-Tom at 431 South Armstrong and the Pig at 505. There were other places where the young liked to "hang out" — especially the root beer stands around town. None, however, had the aplomb of the two major drive-ins.

Today's electronic gadgets by which a food or drink order is given to an unseen voice didn't exist at the Tom-Tom and White Pig. Car hops in short skirts or tights (some on roller skates) took the

The old Exposition Hall was a favorite recreation center for many years.
— Drawing by Dr. H. D. Morgan

order at the window on the driver's side, delivered it moments later on a tray that hooked securely on the car door, then returned to pick it up when the horn was honked or the headlights flashed.

This, of course, was before television and air-conditioning turned people into stay-at-homes. Until these inventions came to virtually every household, the great outside was a magnet in good weather. There were weekly concerts in the park by the Municipal Band. Labor unions and fraternal groups held regular family dinners in their halls. And, if there were nothing else to do, relaxing in the front porch swing or visiting with neighbors in the front yards got almost everyone outside during the early evening hours.

A Palm Garden and Jellybean Corner

Downtown was where everybody went on Saturdays and evenings. Thompson's Drug Store, which boasted the biggest soda fountain in town, was a destination for boys hoping to meet girls. Young men, most wearing the straw sailor hats that were popular then, stood in knots in front of Thompson's to ogle the young ladies passing by. Everybody knew the spot as "Jellybean Corner."

A competitor for the younger crowd, especially during the "flapper" era, was Tony's Palm Garden, also on Main Street. It not only claimed to have the best soda fountain in town, but also an interior "garden" sporting palm trees and ferns and looking like an ersatz tropical island. In addition to a full line of cigarettes (everybody smoked then), Tony displayed two live alligators imported from Louisiana.

From the days of the shoddy ballrooms that dotted Skiddy Street in the town's infancy, dancing has been a popular pastime. In the big band era of the 1940's, the more affluent went to Tropical Gardens. A former chicken hatchery on old U.S. 75 at the south edge of town, it had been converted into an excellent restaurant which featured one-night stands by bands like those of Tommy Dorsey, Russ Morgan and others. On Saturday nights, Denison

Getting there was half the fun on these open electric cars that could make forty miles an hour on straight track.
— *Chamber of Commerce*

attracted the radio listeners of the entire nation when Station KRRV fed the 300 stations of the Mutual Broadcasting System thirty minutes of such music.

In those days, the author of this book was a part-time announcer on KRRV and sometimes his assignment was to introduce the national show with these words:

"Good evening, ladies and gentlemen all across America. We are greeting you from the beautiful and far-famed Tropical Gardens in Denison, where Texas dances under the stars."

For the crowd that preferred beer to wine and set-ups (one carried his own liquor into Tropical Gardens in a paper sack), and country western to the big bands, there was Locust Row on the East Texas Street road. Locally it had the undeserved name of "honky tonk." Actually it was a place that catered to all ages who enjoyed the toe-tapping music of Haskell Rannals and His Dixie Rhythm Boys (who also did thirty-minute shows on KRRV).

Carnivals, the Circus and the Roller Bowl

If dancing wasn't in the plan, there was Curley O'Donnell's Roller Bowl on Main Street, where parents could bowl on one floor while their children skated on another. And there were the circuses that came to town (even Ringling Bros. & Barnum & Bailey had Denison on its schedule for years). And the carnival sponsored by the Lions Club to raise money for children's causes was an annual event. Other groups like the American Legion also brought in an occasional carnival with a ferris-wheel and a variety of rides and shows.

Those times (except for the Lions carnival) are gone with the passing parade. Their memory, however, lingers on.

One diversion that began when Main Street was laid out and trains began arriving at the Katy station has persisted for almost a century and a quarter. That is what the young crowd today calls "cruisin'" and was a favorite pastime of young couples in buggies before the automobile arrived. In the 1950's, teenagers driving cars up and down the main drag of an evening became a kind of fad and still is popular. In fact, Denison aspires (as noted below) to become the "cruisin' capital" of the world as another way of revitalizing Main Street.

A Special Time for the *Texas Special*

Whatever the conveyance, driving up and down Main is a pleasantry enjoyed by all ages. Watching the evening trains come in was almost a rite for three-quarters of a century. In the early days, buggies, wagons and even riders on horseback converged at the depot at train time. After automobiles came into vogue, the parking lot on the south side of Main was always filled. Dozens would be double parked in the street.

Few were there to board the train or to meet arriving passengers. It was thrill enough to be only spectators who loved to watch the Katy's big Pacific steam locomotives come roaring into the station, yellow flame spurting from their fireboxes and warm steam rising from their exhausts. Greeting the northbound *Texas Special* as it arrived about dusk was the highpoint of the day.

By then the lights were always on in the Pullman coaches, and it was the beginning of the dinner hour in the diner. To those on the depot platform or sitting in their cars, the tables with their white linen cloths, candles and gleaming silver and the waiters in their jackets provided a panorama of which the watchers never tired. After a twenty-minute pause to change crews, the great, bright wonderful train was off to distant places like St. Louis, Washington, and New York, and it would be another day before the scene was repeated.

As the observation car disappeared up the tracks, the onlookers would start their motors and perform the second ritual of the evening — a cruise up Main Street. If it were a Saturday night when the stores didn't close until 9:00 P.M., the trick was to find a place to park and "people watch." The 200 block was a favorite spot because of its three movie houses, the Double Dip Ice Cream Store, Mike Patti's Confectionery, a pool hall and other interesting attractions.

The shops no longer are open and the theaters have moved to suburban malls, but "cruisin'" in 1991 was more popular than ever. In fact, some believe that it could be the key to the revitalization of Main Street.

In 1988, the Chamber of Commerce Tourism Committee, anxious to attract more visitors to downtown, adopted Louis Pollaro's idea of trying to develop Denison into the "Cruisin' Capital of the World." His plan won wide support from other civic leaders such as David Bayless, Jr., chairman of the city tourism committee.

Making Main an "Electric Avenue"

The idea will take time to develop, but Pollaro is confident that it will succeed. Denison's Main still resembles a business street of the 1950's so accurately that Pollaro has used it as a set for making the national television commercials and backgrounds for movie scenes that his company produces. To convert it into the "Electric Avenue" he foresees would require the initial restoration of several buildings to their 1950's look. Stucco veneer and other "improvements" added over the years would have to go. Traffic would be controlled by officers in a trio of 1950-era police cars that he owns. Double-decker buses would haul visitors up and down the street and from nearby parking areas.

Businesses would include a theater showing movies of the period, an old-fashioned ice cream parlor and a variety of others that were popular in that pre-war decade. As envisioned by the planners, Main would become a "street of dreams" where one could relive an era out of the past.

Such theme streets aren't new of themselves. Branson, Missouri, turned its downtown into a series of country western theaters that annually attract thousands of visitors. The German community of Fredericksburg in the Texas Hill Country has turned its Main Street into a six-block center of historic buildings, craft and antique shops. The town (population 7,000) hosts well over 100,000 visitors each year.

Pollaro and others believe that Denison, by welcoming cruisin' and restoring Main Street much like it was forty years ago, can become a unique entertainment center that will attract fanciers of old automobiles, railroad buffs, Eisenhower admirers, fishermen and myriad other visitors. That, the planners believe, will bring back good times in the old town again.

15

Casting Call

"In the street of By-and-By
Stands the hostelry of Never.
Dream from deed he must dissever
Who his fortune here would try."
— William Ernest Henley (1849–1903)

The name "Denison" rarely appears in the entertainment news coming out of Hollywood and the Broadway theater. Yet the town has made some significant contributions to the history of both stage and screen.

For example, there were the three singing brothers who, because they made a Denison audience laugh, went on to become the most famous family comedy team in theatrical history. And what of the chunky, mischievous grade school kid who became a star in the most successful series of movie comedies ever produced?

Many Denisonians who bought their gasoline at a particular station never knew that the owner was the first dancing partner of a Texas girl who would go on to international fame as a movie star. And if it had not been for the daughter of a Katy crew dispatcher in Denison, the greatest movie hit of all time might never have been produced.

They Laughed When the Brothers Stood Up to Sing

The two days spent in Denison by a song and dance trio of brothers in the 1920's would change their lives and make them internationally famous. It would be the most important stop they ever made as their career moved along the street of By-and-By. Vaudeville was in its prime then, and success on the circuit of tank town theaters was the route to New York.

There were five brothers in this remarkable family, but only three siblings were aiming at Broadway. Their specialty was a singing and dancing act which also included a female performer, and their director and manager was the boys' Aunt Hannah. They had been well-received in their Texas appearances, although the lady singer seemed to be perpetually off-key. Except for occasional changes in the music, however, the show hadn't varied — until it was booked into the Denison Opera House for matinee and evening shows on Friday and Saturday. They had been hired as a special feature to entertain a convention of school teachers meeting at the time.

Although their music apparently had its charms, the theater manager decided that four such shows would leave a sour note with the audience. He insisted that they omit the singing and do a comedy sketch each evening — a change for which he offered them $100, an astounding figure at the time.

Money became the mother of invention, and a humorous sketch called "Fun In Hi Skule" was born. Aunt Hannah and the girl vocalist were the students; the elder brother was the teacher and another a scholar with a German accent. The third brother, with his boyish looks and a rather vacant expression, became the half-witted country moron. Costumes and props were hard to come by on short notice, but the class dummy was identified by a dirty red wig made of cotton and frayed pieces of rope by Aunt Hannah.

The new act was such a hit in Denison that it was repeated when the group moved on to Nacogdoches (which also alleges to be the place where the team got its start — a claim denied in a biography written by the son of one of the performers). As the troupe rolled across Texas, the show was applauded at every stop and soon it was attracting national attention. The Marx Brothers were on their way to

The Denison Opera House, 100 block West Woodard, owned by M. L. Epstein, is believed to be the theater in which the Marx Brothers first performed the comedy skit that would make them world famous.

becoming the nation's most loved family comedy team. Groucho, Gummo and Harpo — the three who originated the show — were joined later by Chico and Zeppo, and the original sketch was expanded into movies, radio and television shows and stage performances.

One thing, however, never changed. Harpo later acquired a floppy tan coat, an auto horn and a cane. But the red wig he wore that night in Denison remained a part of his stage costume until his death.

The Kid Next Door

Everybody at one time or another has known a cute, fat precocious child like Spanky McFarland.

He could have lived next door to any family on any street in town. His friends would have been kids like freckle-faced Alfalfa and a half dozen others of the kind that peopled the fourth and fifth grade classes at Central Ward or Peabody Schools in the early 1930's. And it's almost certain that they would have used somebody's barn or storage shed as a club house for their "gang."

Where Spanky McFarland actually lived has been lost, but he was born in Denison and spent his early years there. And he went on to star in "Our Gang" comedies, probably the most popular movie series about kids ever to come out of Hollywood.

The comedies continued to be made for a few years after McFarland outgrew his role and still are shown today as television re-runs. After his career as the chunky, lovable child star, McFarland went on to other endeavors and never returned to his old hometown.

He Danced with Ginger

Another stage star had his name in lights long before Denison became his home. He was Buck Williams, a gasoline distributor and service station operator after he moved to Denison. Most of his customers in the 1940's never knew that the likeable Williams preceded Fred Astaire as the first dancing partner of Ginger Rogers.

Like Miss Rogers, Williams was a native of Fort Worth and had red hair. Again like the winsome Ginger, he started his career as a professional dancer after winning a Charleston contest in his home town when he was sixteen. Miss Rogers' age at the time isn't known.

In 1926, after Miss Rogers won the state Charleston championship, she decided to take her show on the road. She signed young Williams as her partner. For almost two years, Ginger Rogers and Her Red Heads (in addition to Rogers and Williams the troupe included five auburn-haired girls) toured the entire country on the old Keith-Orpheum Vaudeville Circuit. Then Williams quit, formed his own dance team and continued as a stage star until the movies killed live vaudeville. That's when he moved to Denison and started his oil business.

The Bus Boy Who Hit the Big Time

A well-known face on television today belongs to sixty-six-year-old Melvin Bryant, a 1942 graduate of the old Terrell High School who still calls Denison home. He still visits old friends in Denison when he isn't entertaining in Las Vegas shows or on cruise ships or making movies. He has been the pitchman in dozens of TV commercials.

Melvin has come a long way since his first job of using his brother's portable stand to shine shoes for a nickel.

Bryant, whose father was an alcoholic, was raised by an aunt. He says he has no idea what might have happened to him except for the late Edna Davis. She took him under her wing, paid him $2.50 per week to do odd jobs around her Post Office Drug Store, and called a taxi every day to see that he got to school. The driver was instructed to wait until Melvin actually went inside.

Miss Davis also served lunches in her little store in the 100 block of North Rusk and Melvin began singing for patrons who had a birthday. His tip was a nickel. The money he earned was important, but the philosophy Miss Davis instilled in him was more so.

"Miss Edna taught me that there was no difference between whites and blacks," Bryant told *Herald* editor Donna Hunt on a visit home in the summer of 1991. "She said it's the way you carry yourself that matters. One day I asked her, 'Why do people hate us?' and she told me that no one is better than anyone else."

Bryant's success in the entertainment world was a happenstance. In 1943, he had an opportunity to go to California by sharing expenses with his next door neighbor, Ray Frazier, a black undertaker. It cost him $15, but he hoped he could get a good job in the Long Beach shipyards. Instead he took a job as a busboy in a Los Angeles cafeteria patronized by wealthy society people. The place had an organ, and when a tune that he knew was played, Melvin sometimes sang as he cleared tables. The customers liked that.

The organist, noting the reaction to Melvin's singing, invited him one night to sing as a part of the entertainment. An agent for actors was dining there that evening, heard Melvin and asked him to come to his home the next day. It seems that Metro-Goldwyn-Mayor had been looking for an actor to play the role of a black shoeshine boy in a movie role. Melvin got the part and the unbelievable salary (to him) of $250 a week.

However, he already had planned to enlist in the Marines and he left the movie set after two weeks. Fate still smiled on him, however, and when he returned to Hollywood after sixteen months in uniform, MGM loaned him to 20th Century Fox and then to RKO for a movie called "Riverboat Rhythm." He appeared in several others and had a singing role in the film version of "Porgy and Bess."

Today he is often seen in television commercials for major companies like McDonald's, Lipton's Soup, Maxwell House Coffee and others. He also tries to do a show or two each year on cruise ships. And he still likes to get back to Denison and visit with old friends.

She Sold Hollywood What It Didn't Want

Melvin Bryant never knew Annie Laurie Williams, but in her time, her name was as well known among Hollywood producers as any big name star. In fact, she was a star in her own right, but not on the stage, as she had hoped, or the screen.

Annie Laurie was a literary agent. By selling Hollywood producers stories they didn't want at prices unheard of before, she became, perhaps, the nation's best-known and most successful individual in her field. She not only made a fortune for herself, but she turned the names of many struggling, unknown writers into household words by persuading Hollywood to turn their works into some of the most memorable motion pictures of all time.

This was never her intention while growing up in the 200 block of West Munson Street in Denison. Her father, P. E. Williams, was a crew dispatcher for the Katy Railroad. To his blonde and beautiful

Melvin Bryant used to shine shoes in Denison for a nickel. Now he counts among his Hollywood friends such celebrities as the late Sammy Davis, Jr.

— Photo courtesy of Melvin Bryant

Annie Laurie Williams made a fortune selling Hollywood stories for the movies that it didn't want.
— *Collection of the Author*

daughter, it was the kind of boring job that could only inspire her to leave at her first opportunity what she regarded as a dingy railroad town.

As the chief dispatcher, her father was in charge of calling train and engine crews to report to work. He personally called the few such workers who had telephones. Most, however, didn't have phones in this era of the Great Depression. To alert these engineers, firemen, conductors and brakemen that an assignment awaited, Williams had a staff of "call boys" who went to workers' homes and delivered the message. At best, their jobs provided only a living, and not a very good one. To Annie Laurie, this was the kind of unglamorous work typical of life in a small town. She set her goals on New York and/or Hollywood.

After high school, she headed for New York, where she got a few minor acting roles. Frustrated and disappointed, she sought another way into the entertainment business. An avid reader, she felt that many good new novels were being overlooked by Hollywood as potential hit movies. She decided to try to sell producers stories they apparently didn't want. She became an author's agent.

One day she picked up a book written by a Presbyterian preacher and issued by a small publisher of religious works. She read it, liked it and decided it would make a successful movie. She took it to several producers, each of whom rejected it on sight. Undaunted, she kept showing it around until one movie company, wanting to be rid of her, agreed to take a second look. A few months later, *The Magnificent Obsession* became one of the hit movies of the year. It was the first of a succession of best-selling books that came from the prolific pen of Lloyd C. Douglas. But Hollywood snubbed him until Miss Williams came along.

That was the beginning of a career that made Annie Laurie internationally known as the agent who specialized in selling Hollywood stories that it didn't want, often before they were published as books.

Name almost any famous author of the 1940's and 1950's and Annie Laurie Williams was their agent. It was she who talked Hollywood into filming Alice Hobart's *Oil for the Lamps of China* and Taylor Caldwell's *This Side of Innocence*. Without her help, Ben Ames Williams' *Leave Her to Heaven* and John Hersey's *A Bell for Adano* might never have reached the silver screen. Alfred Noyes and Paul Gallico and John Steinbeck all were her clients. So was Kathleen Windsor, author of the controversial *Forever Amber*.

It was Annie Laurie Williams who sold John Steinbeck's *The Moon Is Down* to the movies for $300,000 — the highest price ever paid for motion picture rights up to that time. She also sold the movie rights to his *Of Mice and Men*. Producers rejected Steinbeck's *Grapes of Wrath* at first, claiming it was too realistic to film. Annie Laurie finally convinced them to do it anyway, and it became a movie classic.

As her reputation grew, she found it easier to persuade producers to trust her judgment in selecting books that were potential hit movies. There was one, however, she thought that she would never sell.

It was a bulky manuscript — longer than most novels — written by a young Georgia matron. It had not been published in book form when she began lugging the manuscript around to movie producers. Each took one look and said a resounding "no."

Finally she got the manuscript to David O. Selznick, the twelfth producer to see it. He didn't really like it, but Annie Laurie convinced him to take a chance for $50,000. He bought it.

It was *Gone with the Wind*, a smash success both as a book and a film starring Clark Gable and Vivien Leigh. It became the greatest box office success of all time. More than half a century later, videotapes sell for about $90 each, and movie theaters all over the world still show it.

As this is written, a "sequel" to *Gone with the Wind* is being published. The original author, Margaret Mitchell, is dead. So are the principal stars of the movie. If the sequel turns out to be a best-seller, it may or may not become a movie.

That's because Annie Laurie Williams, who died several years ago, won't be around to talk a producer into buying the motion picture rights to a book he doesn't want.

Big Name on the Small Screen

Fans of the hit television show "Magnum PI" invariably type John Hillerman, the sophisticated sidekick of Tom Selleck, as British. With his clipped accent, mustache and cool demeanor, he looks and talks like the master of an English country estate. Only those who have read his publicity know that he was born in the unsophisticated railroad town in Texas named Denison, the son of the owner of a gasoline service station.

Hillerman wanted to be an actor even when he was a student at St. Xavier's Academy. On graduation, he attended The University of Texas at Austin for three years and then did a four-year stint in the Air Force. During his years in uniform he worked with various theatrical groups, and on his discharge, he went to New York to study at the American Theatre Wing. In 1957, he began his career in professional theater as the resident juvenile at the Chatauqua Playhouse in Middleton, Ohio.

From that point on, his career as an actor has been meteoric.

16

The Big Red

"I do not know much about gods; but I think that the river
Is a strong brown god — sullen, untamed and intractable."
— Thomas Stearns Eliot

The Red River has never been called beautiful. It is ugly. It is mischievous. Whereas other rivers are placid and inspire poets to write sonnets about them, the Red is "sullen, untamed and intractable." It is treacherous, dangerous, deceptive and unpredictable.

It also is Denison's greatest pride and most lasting disappointment.

The town's pride comes from the huge earthen dam (one of the largest of its kind in the world when it was completed in 1944) and the magnificent 95,000-acre Lake Texoma, the tenth largest reservoir in the country. In a given year, some eleven million people visit the lake to boat, fish, hunt and enjoy the beautiful resorts that dot its 1,251-mile shoreline.

Denison Dam and the lake have made Denison, once known primarily for its railroads, a tourist mecca. Although its beautiful Union Station hasn't served a passenger train since 1965, travelers come by the thousands by automobile, bus and planes to visit Lake Texoma and, hopefully, pause awhile on historic Main Street. The town is proud of the changes the river has brought.

Nevertheless an aura of disappointment lingers, particularly with the old-timers who know something of Denison's history. The founders in 1872 really had two goals: to make the place a railroad hub and also an important river port. The latter dream never came true.

The river has always defied efforts to navigate its muddy water. In 1690, when Domingo Teran de los Rios and his Spanish explorers came through northeast Texas, they discovered that the Red was clogged for miles by the biggest woodpile ever seen in North America. The Caddo Indians, who had roamed north Louisiana and East Texas for centuries, called this driftwood obstruction "the Great Raft." They said it had been there forever.

Even this barrier, eventually more than 150 miles long, could not stop all river traffic. As the raft formed, the Red escaped its channel and made new bayous and shallow lakes. Somehow steamboats were able to maneuver around the debris and get as far north as Shreveport, Louisiana, and Jefferson, Texas. A few, in fact, made it all the way to Coffey's Trading Post at Preston Bend, only a few miles from the site of Denison today.

Steamboat 'Round the Bend

Forty years before the first Denison lots were sold, the U.S. government began trying to clear the Red of its impediment. The job cost more than a million dollars and was completed in 1873 as Denison was about to celebrate its first birthday. With the Great Raft gone and the river declared navigable from its mouth to Preston Bend, many of the settlers believed steamboats would be arriving any day.

Actually, small cargo boats had been steaming up the river to Preston when Denison was still just an idea in the mind of Katy Railroad planners. On December 15, 1902, more than thirty years after the town's founding, a steamboat captain named Joe Briary swore under oath that he had piloted a sternwheeler to Preston often in the late 1860's and early 1870's.

However, it wasn't until April 21, 1905, that the 105-foot, twin-stacked *Annie P.* docked at Denison and brought renewed hope of a river port. The steamer carried seventy-one tons of cargo and could navigate in as little as two feet of water. The *Annie*

The arrival of the steamboat, the *Annie P.*, in 1905 rekindled the dreams that the Red River could be navigated and that Denison would become an inland port.

P. made another voyage to Denison later in the summer, then became a Louisiana excursion boat. Abused and neglected, eventually it sank while docked.

Although these voyages proved that bringing boats upriver was possible, it was too costly and risky to be practical. The unpredictable Red did not maintain a uniform depth or channel from one day to the next.

Still the dream of someday making Denison a river port remained. Dr. Alex W. Acheson, early physician and mayor, never lost the hope that one day cargo boats would be tied up at docks along the river. Preaching the gospel of Red River navigation became to him second only to the practice of medicine. He ran unsuccessfully for Congress, hoping he could take that message to Washington.

Although his efforts failed, part of his dream came true. In 1945, two navy landing craft made it all the way from New Orleans to Denison as a publicity promotion for the sale of war bonds.

The Last Civil War?

This effort at navigation was not to come, however, until after the river had been the scene of what some historians have described as "the last war between the states." Indeed, in 1931, Texas and Oklahoma turned both the north and south banks of the big Red into a battleground over a toll bridge north of Denison.

Fortunately for the Texas forces, the nine-day siege was bloodless and shotless. The military odds they faced were even greater than those of the defenders of the Alamo almost a century earlier. In the argument with Oklahoma, the Lone Star State fielded six Texas Rangers, the Grayson County sheriff and four deputies. Their only arms were Colt .45 revolvers.

Oklahoma sent five companies of its best National Guards to the site. One boasted a machine gun platoon. They also mounted one howitzer.

Each "army" had a separate objective as they

World War Soldiers Deserve a Bonus
Vote for
ACHESON for CONGRESS

Dr. Alex W. Acheson ran for Congress, but lost.
— *Ralph Douglas Collection*

dug in on opposite banks of the river. The Texas Rangers' assignment was to keep traffic on U.S. 75 from using a just completed toll-free bridge. Oklahoma's guards were there to stop traffic from entering the Sooner State over a Texas-owned toll bridge that stood a few hundred yards downriver from the new span.

The net result was that traffic on the heavily traveled highway that stretches from Galveston to Winnipeg, Canada, came to a grinding halt. It remained stalled until the governors of the two states and the federal courts got both bridges open and called their warriors home. However, the basic point at issue — whether individuals have the right to build bridges across streams and charge the fees for their use — has never been settled satisfactorily.

The Texas-Oklahoma "war" was precipitated years before when the highway commissions of both states agreed to free all toll bridges on the Red River by purchasing the spans from their owners. Stockholders of three of the bridges — those connecting Gainesville, Texas, and Marietta, Oklahoma; Ringgold, Texas, and Terral, Oklahoma; and Denison and Colbert, Oklahoma — refused to sell.

The two states responded by agreeing to build free bridges at these points. Then owners of the toll spans sued to prevent this action. When they lost in the courts, investors in the Denison-Colbert span agreed to sell for $60,000, payable when the parallel free bridge was operational. They also demanded the right to increase tolls while the new project was building. If the new span was completed in less than fourteen months, the toll owners demanded $10,000 additional for each month in which they had not been able to charge motorists.

The War Department Creates a War

Texas authorities agreed. However, the U.S. Department of Defense (War Department in those days) has control of all navigable streams. Although it is arguable that the Red River is navigable, the Feds denied the request for the increased tolls.

In January 1931, the new free bridge was almost completed. The owners of the Denison-Colbert span went back to court demanding $60,000 from Texas, plus another $30,000 in tolls they claimed to have lost after the War Department refused their request to increase rates. A Houston federal judge issued an injunction preventing the opening of the new free bridge and ordered it barricaded on the Texas approach.

William H. (Alfalfa Bill) Murray, Oklahoma's governor at the time, was a native of Collin County, Texas. (His birthplace, known as Toadsuck, has disappeared.) He didn't like a judge in his native state interfering in a matter affecting Oklahoma. Besides he had promised the people of Oklahoma that he would make all Red River crossings toll free. He intended to keep that promise.

By July 16, the Okie leader had had enough. He sent three of his Highway Department employees to drive over the new bridge and take down the Texas barricades. They did, and traffic began streaming across the bridge from both sides of the river.

In Austin, Governor Ross S. Sterling exploded at what he considered an affront to both a federal court and to Texas. He dispatched Rangers to Denison to reconstruct the barricades and enforce the blockade with a round-the-clock guard.

Murray's Version of "The Iron Curtain"

Again it was "Alfalfa Bill's" move. He countered by ordering his troops of infantry to the scene. Not wanting to risk a confrontation with the Texas Rangers by once again attempting to remove the entrance barriers, Murray deployed a different of-

In the "last war between the states," four Texas Rangers protect the new toll-free Red River bridge against a company of Oklahoma National Guard.

— Photo by Claud Easterly

The first barrier erected at the new bridge didn't stay long. It was removed on orders of Oklahoma Governor William H. (Alfalfa Bill) Murray, a native Texan who almost went to war with his home state.

— Photo by Claud Easterly

During the Red River war, Oklahoma guardsmen also closed the Carpenter's Bluff toll bridge to traffic.
— *Frontier Village Museum Photo*

fense. His guardsmen plowed up the highway leading to the Oklahoma entrance to the toll bridge. This action effectively closed both spans and stopped all traffic at that point between the two states.

For three days, the bloodless battle continued with neither side giving in and hundreds of stalled motorists and truckers fuming. When Governor Murray heard that some were detouring six miles downriver and crossing on the toll bridge owned by the Kansas, Oklahoma & Gulf Railroad at Carpenter's Bluff, he ordered his forces to plow up the road to that span also.

Murray, who loved a good fight, made a field inspection to the battlefield and set up his own GHQ in a tent. He issued orders that the bridges were to be defended "against all authority except the President of the United States." Apparently the White House was more concerned with finding a solution to the Great Depression that had the nation in its grip. At least, President Herbert Hoover took no action.

But Judge T. M. Kennerly, who had issued the injunction, did. On July 25, he ordered Texas to remove the barricades to the free bridge. One of the first cars to cross it was a black limousine carrying the triumphant governor of Oklahoma.

The Texas Rangers went home. The Oklahoma Guard refused to leave, however, because Judge Kennerly had not made the dissolution of the injunction permanent. This he finally did on August 6 and the guardsmen went back to their workaday jobs in Oklahoma. The Red River bridges were forever free of tolls, and the "war" was over.

Legal battles, however, would continue for another seven years until both Oklahoma and Texas

When travelers continued to use the toll bridge over the Red River, Governor Murray stopped all traffic by plowing up the Oklahoma highway leading to the span.

— *Frontier Village Museum photo*

finally agreed to make financial settlements with the toll span owners.

The last "war between the states" made headlines across the nation. It was not until construction of the huge Denison Dam and the creation of Lake Texoma began that the river once again got such notice from the national media.

In fact, until the possibility of a giant flood control dam became more than a dream, the Red River had never attracted much attention except from those who hoped that it could be navigable. One of these visionaries was George D. Moulton, who became convinced as early as 1926 that an earthen dam at Denison would forever halt the disastrous floods that often created havoc downstream.

Best Town in Texas by a Damsite

Moulton was a youngster when he arrived in Denison with his father in 1872. He was the adopted son of J. B. McDougall, builder of one of the town's famous opera houses. Moulton became interested in flood control early on and spent much of his life trying to convince the federal government that the Red River needed to be dammed.

Although Dr. Acheson was an advocate of navigation rather than a dam, he had paved the way for Moulton's later efforts. Acheson, who believed that river traffic would make Denison the center of "the greatest inland empire in the world," had even addressed the U.S. Senate on the subject. Thus many members of Congress already knew of Denison and the town's interest in Red River development when Moulton began writing letters to them. One — Representative Charles D. Carter of Oklahoma — sent him contour maps of the area, and Moulton selected a site that is now roughly the Lake Texoma Basin.

In 1927, the first proposal for a Denison Reservoir, as it was called, went before Congress. Gradually the idea of a flood control dam on the river at Denison gained momentum, but it was nine years before Congress sent engineers to make a pre-

George P. Moulton, credited with being the "father" of the Denison Dam, poses here at the site where construction began.

— *Frontier Village Museum*

liminary survey. The first appropriation of $5.6 million came in 1939 and provided that the dam would be designed to generate electricity as well as to control floods.

There were still obstacles to overcome. Governor Leon C. Phillips of Oklahoma opposed the project because it would inundate more than 100,000 acres of his state, and he had not been assured of remuneration to replace roads and other facilities. The Supreme Court ruled against him, and construction began.

To direct the project, the U.S. Army Engineers sent a young captain, Lucius D. Clay, to Denison and the district office for that branch of the service was placed under his command. Soon building a dam became almost a secondary project. With a war in the offing, the Denison office was suddenly assigned new responsibilities. Its staff designed and directed the construction of Sheppard Air Force Base at Wichita Falls, Perrin AFB between Denison and Sherman, Eaker Field at Durant and other facilities.

Meanwhile preparation of the dam construction site was started. Before its completion, it would become one of the largest land-clearing projects in American history. In one way, the war proved a boon.

War Prisoners Helped

Work was still in progress in 1943 with the conflict overseas in full stride. Thousands of prisoners of war had been taken and interned at camps in the U.S. Two such detention centers were in Oklahoma at points near the damsite. These unwilling guests of our government were put to work chopping down trees, re-routing roads and similar chores.

German prisoners of war, who had been captured by the British in North Africa, got the assignment to do most of it. They cleared more than 7,000 acres during their enforced stay in the area.

The war also cut short the tenure of Captain Clay. In the fall of 1940, he was transferred to Washington and began a quick rise in the military ranks. He would go to Europe as an aide to Denison's native son, Dwight D. Eisenhower, then the U.S. deputy military commander of occupied Germany. And it would be Clay who, in 1948, organized the Berlin Airlift that broke the Soviet blockade. He retired as a four-star general and became a senior partner of the mortgage banking firm of Lehman Brothers in New York. He never returned to see the project that he had started in Denison.

After Clay left, various heads of the Army Engineers directed the construction of the dam. When completed, it would be one of the largest earthen dams built up to that time in the world. The sheer size of the project boggles the imagination.

Making Way for Texas' Biggest Lake

Miles of railroad tracks and highways had to be relocated. Some 3,000 graves had to be moved from forty-nine different cemeteries in the area. More than three million cubic feet of dirt had to be

World War II prisoners of war relax in their camp after working on Denison Dam project. Chess game pawns on the table in front of them were censored by U.S. Army Intelligence officers because they feared they might contain a message for the enemy.

— *Photo by Claud Easterly*

excavated just to house the encased conduits that stretch below the finished dam. Another 11.5 million cubic yards had to be gouged from what had been a flat strip of country to provide for the spillway.

Moving what literally was a mountain of earth gave Denison a new, unique and short-lived industry. The building at 619 West Main, now occupied by the Lone Star Gas Company, became a truck assembly plant!

To transport the tons of earth that had to be moved in the construction of the dam, the contractor needed trucks of a size never built before. So engineers designed the "Goliaths," as they were called, and had a Kentucky company manufacture the parts. Everything — motors, transmissions, wheels, frames, cabs, etc. — was shipped to Denison and assembled in the Main Street "factory." Eventually seventeen of the earth-movers were assembled before the plant closed.

Some seventeen million cubic yards of earth went into the dam itself. So did an incredible amount of cement. The outlet works alone required 240,000 cubic yards of concrete — enough to build a highway ninety-one miles long.

When Congress approved the original appropriation for the Denison Dam, hundreds of residents staged an impromptu parade on Main Street.

Congressman Rayburn inspects the damsite with Captain Lucius D. Clay, the U.S. Army engineer who was the first director of the project. Clay later became a four-star general and one of the important figures in WWII.

Congressman Sam Rayburn, who pushed the appropriation for Denison Dam through Congress, visits the damsite.
— Claud Easterly photo

Even ice — fourteen million tons of it — went into the construction. It seems that the large masses of concrete would shrink and develop internal stress unless the temperature of the mix was kept around fifty degrees. Care had to be taken to figure the moisture content of the ice and the water used in the cement mixture, and the amount of sand proportionately reduced.

With a war on, petroleum was especially precious and Oklahoma's Cumberland oil field northwest of Madill had to be protected. A huge dike was built to keep the lake behind the new dam from inundating the 11.5 square miles of producing wells.

Below the dam itself, a powerhouse was built to produce the electricity generated by the thundering flow of river water. It required a massive structure fifteen stories high, 160 feet long and 70 feet wide. To those driving over the road that crosses the dam today, the powerhouse appears smaller only because 84 feet of its 150-foot height is below ground.

Water Everywhere — but No Steamboats

Building Denison Dam and creating Lake Texoma put Denison's railroads to the test. More than two thousand 100-car freight trains hauled in the materials and machinery. The job required twenty-three million man hours of labor and cost the lives of twenty-one workers. At capacity, the lake will hold 2,000,000,000,000 gallons of water.

The dam itself is just under three miles in length. When completed, the project had cost $55,250,000.

The structure was formally dedicated on July 1, 1944, with Congressman Sam Rayburn — the man most responsible for guiding the bill creating the Denison Dam through Congress — as the principal speaker. Rayburn, in his dedicatory address, expressed pardonable pride in the Denison Dam project — the only major public work in the nation that was allowed to continue during the war. And he predicted that it would become a great resort

To construct the Denison Dam, it was necessary to build a temporary pontoon bridge across the river.
— *Frontier Village Museum*

area, which it has.

The dam also revived hopes for making the big Red navigable as far as Denison. One more attempt was made in 1945.

This resulted from a publicity stunt staged by the Higgins Boat Company, which manufactured small boats for the U.S. Navy. It sent two of its landing craft — one for personnel and one for mechanized equipment — to prove that the river was navigable by shallow-draft vessels. They made it as far as Honey Grove, Fannin County, when the boats went aground. They probably would still be imbedded in the sand there except for the fact that the Denison Dam had been completed and was functioning.

Army engineers released enough water to enable the boats to push their way on to Denison. No attempts to navigate the river to Denison have been made since.

Apparently Mr. Rayburn didn't believe that navigation would be a reality. At least he didn't touch on it in his dedicatory speech. Neither did he predict how the dam, and its mammoth lake, would also change the face and character of what once was called "the meanest river in Texas."

It was that and more in 1872, when the Katy rails spanned it and entered Texas. Then it was a dreaded stream of quicksand, feared by the trail

This aerial photograph shows how what was then the second largest earthen dam in the world looked on its completion in 1944 at a cost of $55,250,000.

— U.S. Corps of Army Engineers Photo

drivers trying to get their cattle across, and hated by those who lived along its mosquito-filled shores. More than that, it was a psychological barrier to Texans who resented the fact that not one of its sandbars belonged to Texas. Years before, the Supreme Court had ruled that Oklahoma and Texas do not share ownership of the big Red. The Oklahoma state line extends to the *south* bank, making the river the sole property of that state.

Building the Denison Dam and the creation of Lake Texoma hasn't changed the boundary situation, which still irks most Texans. But these two man-made marvels altered the face of the river for miles downstream. Its waters no longer are mud red, but are as blue as the Texas sky. Its banks, which were undesirable for building because of the river's oft-changing channels, are now the site of beautiful homes, fine resorts, fishing camps, parks and restaurants. It still isn't a Thames or a Seine or a Danube. It isn't even a River Jordan, although religious groups still occasionally risk the quicksand and undertows and baptize there. Newcomers — those who have chosen to make their homes in Texomaland since the lake finally filled to capacity in 1945 — cannot have a sense of what the big Red used to be.

One characteristic of the mean, capricious stream has not changed and never shall. Known to Indian tribes for centuries before it was discovered by the Spanish more than 300 years ago, the big Red always has been a river of history. This it will continue to be for generations yet unborn.

17

Into the Wild, Blue Yonder

"Our hopes, like towering falcons, aim
At objects in an airy height;
The little pleasure of the game
Is from afar to view the flight."
— Matthew Prior (1664–1721)

Denison may be the child of a railroad, but aviation also has contributed a great deal to the history of the town.

It was, if one can believe contemporary newspaper accounts, one of the first communities in Texas to report seeing a "flying saucer." That was only six years after the town was founded.

On July 4, 1906, while many residents were off riding Katy excursion trains to celebrate Independence Day, hundreds of others were at home watching a daredevil ascend in a home-made balloon.

Five years later, on October 17, 1911, an estimated 5,000 people (half the town's population) turned out to greet the first airplane ever to fly over Denison. Calbraith Perry Rodgers brought the wild, blue yonder to earthbound Grayson County when he followed the Katy tracks to land in Pottsboro.

If Rodgers' flight had been a few years later, he would have had a real airport on which to set down his plane. Denison established its first municipal airfield in the late 1920's. In fact, it was the community's abiding interest in aviation that helped convince the U.S. government to establish Perrin Air Force Base southwest of the city in 1941, five months before the Japanese attack on Pearl Harbor.

Was It a Flying Saucer — or a Joke?

There were no airports in Denison or anywhere else in 1878. Perhaps that's why the report in the Denison *Daily News* of January 25, 1878, did not report the landing of a UFO (Unidentified Flying Object). It only said that one was "sighted."

Even the "sighting" was not near Denison. It was reported by a farmer living six miles north of Dallas. Publication of the story by Editor Murray, however, assured Denison a tiny footnote in history. The town still gets credited (inaccurately) now and then by the media as the "first place in Texas" to report seeing a "flying saucer."

More worthy of inclusion in the annals of aviation than the supposed UFO sighting is a real life event twenty-eight years later that had thousands of witnesses. By that time, ascensions by dare-devils in hot air balloons had become a new national craze, and crowds would gather in any convenient pasture to see the shows. However, the one staged on July 4, 1906, was special.

As thousands watched, one Chet Baldwin did something that would have caused a professional balloonist to stop and reconsider. The non-porous bag of hot air that would lift him skyward had been made at home by Mrs. Fred Luck. Baldwin must have placed his confidence in her name rather than her expertise as a seamstress, because the balloon was made of nothing more stable than 100 yards of unbleached muslin. Once the hot air to inflate the bag had been pumped in, Mrs. Luck hoped that the paraffin with which she had coated it would keep this "fuel" from escaping.

His faith in (Mrs.) luck was justified as Baldwin made his ascension to several hundred feet, then parachuted to the ground as the crowd cheered.

Next Time Take the Train

Balloon flights were old stuff by October 17, 1911, when Calbraith Perry Rodgers showed Denison an honest-to-goodness aeroplane for the first

No photographer was on hand when Calbraith Perry Rodgers brought the first airplane over Denison in 1911. But when the flight was reenacted more than half a century later, Claud Easterly of the Denison *Herald* was on hand to photograph the replica of Rodgers' plane.

time. He called the craft the *Vin-Fiz* because his mission was to advertise a soft drink by that name. Why he picked Pottsboro instead of Denison for the first of his twenty-three planned stops in Texas is a mystery because he used railroads as his guide and Denison had five of them. Actually this created an unanticipated problem.

Rodgers' first Texas stop was but one of sixty-eight he would make on a forty-nine-day flight across the U.S. The Hearst Newspapers had offered $50,000 to the first aviator to cross the continent in less than thirty days, and Rodgers wanted the prize. The Vin-Fiz Company paid him $5 a day for expenses and chartered a special train to accompany him. The train carried a crew of mechanics, spare parts for the plane and thousands of leaflets advertising the new soda pop. Also the railroad was Rodgers' only navigation tool. He simply followed the tracks from one stop to another.

The flight over Denison had been anticipated for days. As the special train preceded Rodgers through town, its whistle tied open, school students rushed from classes to watch from windows and roof-tops. As soon as the plane was sighted flying in from the north, the fire bell was sounded. An estimated 5,000 — half the town's population — waved their greetings as he piloted his Wright Model B plane over downtown and headed west.

His fans on the ground knew that Rodgers might be confused. Denison's five steam railroads and one electric interurban line had tracks fanning out like spokes in a wheel. To guide him through the maze, citizens had laid a long strip of white cloth through Sugar Bottom along the Katy's line to Pottsboro.

From Pottsboro, Rodgers' route was to Whitesboro and then over the Katy tracks to Fort Worth. Nobody had warned him, however, that the Katy split again at Whitesboro with one leg going on west to Wichita Falls. The pilot followed the wrong rails, realized that he was lost and landed in Gainesville to ask directions. He flew on a few miles farther to Bonita, found the Fort Worth & Denver tracks and finally got to "the city where the West begins."

An Airport at Last

Like Rodgers and his *Vin-Fiz,* any pilot landing in Denison until the late 1920's had to find a good pasture or put down on one of the gravel roads around the town. Then, two miles east of the city, the 100-acre Gray Field was created. It was named for R. M. (Dick) Gray, a reporter for the Denison

Even with the electronic gadgetry of World War II, carrier pigeons still were used in communications. At Denison Union Station in the 1940s, a Katy baggage handler releases some of the birds on a training flight.

— *Author's Collection*

Herald who also doubled as city fire marshal for many years. There in 1931, commercial air service to Denison began.

In that pre-jet age, any town the size of Denison that could be served by the small propeller-driven planes in use then could be profitable to an airline. Denison was chosen as a regular stop for Braniff on its route from Tulsa and Oklahoma City to Dallas.

The planes were nothing like the huge airlines of today. Serving Denison for Braniff were metal cabin planes made by Hamilton and those made by Fairchild. They carried only six to eight passengers and one pilot. On landing in Denison, each passenger received souvenir postal cards showing local scenes. It was one of the first efforts by the Chamber of Commerce to encourage tourism.

With the introduction of larger planes like the DC-3, and growing competition among the airlines, commercial flights to Gray Field ended. The airport continued to be used by local pilots as a base for their planes, and it was often utilized by the army. In 1946, new owners leased it, added a snack bar and lounge and improved the landing strips. It became a favorite terminal for those flying to and from Lake Texoma. However, Gray would disappear with the creation of the Grayson County Airport in the 1970's on part of the site of the old Perrin Air Force Base.

Here Comes the Air Force

That famous old flying field was the result of the foresight of Grayson County leaders, the cooperation of the federal government and the gathering clouds of World War II.

The war threat had encouraged county citizens early on to acquire land that could be leased to the government for defense purposes. On June 10, 1941, voters approved issuing $80,000 in bonds for such purpose. Less than a month later, the federal government had signed a lease for the property, and

Aerial view of Perrin Air Force Base.

construction of barracks and flight line buildings began on July 8. By December 7, Pearl Harbor Day, ninety officers and 545 enlisted men were on the post and the first class of aviation cadets was expected late that month.

The Japanese attack changed all of that, and training programs were rushed. Cadets began arriving almost immediately, and instruction in the BT-13 aircraft began. The first class was graduated on February 23, 1942. That same day, the new school was dedicated as "Perrin Field." It honored the late Lt. Col. Elmer D. Perrin, a native of Boerne, Kendall County. He had died in an air crash near Baltimore, Maryland, just a few months before the field named for him began operations.

Perrin's growth was rapid. By December 1942, all available space was in use and its barracks were jammed with 4,280 enlisted men. Special training programs had been ordered and every facility was strained. The normal strength of the base was 2,500 enlisted men and 300 officers. By the time basic pilot training was discontinued in February 1946, more than 10,000 students had been graduated and sent on to advanced stations.

In November 1946, Perrin was deactivated. It was reactivated two years later when the U.S. began a limited mobilization program. After the Korean Conflict began in 1950, Perrin became a base to train interceptor pilots. With the end of that war and the change in defense tactics and techniques, the Air Force found less and less use for a base like Perrin. It was closed June 30, 1971.

Although no longer an important U.S. defense facility, Perrin continues to live on. Grayson County Airport is there. So is the campus of Grayson County College, the Greater Texoma Utility Authority, a regional juvenile detention center and several industries.

There is even hope that one day commercial flights will return to what once was one of this nation's important military air bases.

Meanwhile the airport has become a tourist attraction. In 1990, Harold Hastings, a World War II flying ace and descendant of an old Denison family, presented a $250,000 statue as "a window of time." It is a massive, Renaissance-style sculpture of "Icarus." According to Greek legend, Daedalus and his son, Icarus, became the world's first airmen when they fashioned wings of feathers and wax to escape from the island of Crete.

The statue was executed by William Mozart McVey of Philadelphia, famed for his statue of Winston Churchill, complete with cigar, which stands before the British Embassy in Washington. Hastings, who was at Pearl Harbor when the Japanese attacked, got the idea for the unique work of art at London's Heathrow Airport, which displays a statue of the first two English pilots to fly the Atlantic.

Hastings, who spends his winters in Denison and his summers in Corfu, Greece, was among the first Denisonians to enlist in the Air Corps in World War II. He holds the Distinguished Flying Cross, Silver Star and Air Medal and retired with the permanent rank of major. He then became a pilot for TWA and logged some 29,000 hours flying all over the world.

In his remarks at the dedication of "Icarus" on October 13, 1990, Hastings said: "I would like those astronauts of the future to look back through this window of time to the airmen who started it all."

18

The Tracks Ahead

"Now this is not the end. It is not even the beginning of the end. It is, perhaps, the end of the beginning."

— Winston Churchill, speech at Lord Mayor's Day Luncheon, London, November 10, 1942

On May 16, 1988, when word came from Washington that the Union Pacific had received approval of the Interstate Commerce Commission to purchase the Katy, an unidentified local pundit responded with the last lines of the old nursery rhyme:

When the bough breaks, the cradle will fall,
And down will come baby, cradle and all.

Denison, of course, was no longer the baby that the Katy had brought into the world almost 116 years before. Rather the city was a robust and enduring monument built by men like Robert S. Stevens, W. B. Munson, Sr. and many others — a heritage they had bequeathed to their modern successors.

The valedictory of the parent railroad was a severe economic loss to the community, for the Katy had been a sustaining industry for almost twelve decades. It was also a personal loss to the hundreds who prided themselves on being members of the Katy family. Most, however, had seen signs for years that the railroad was sick and that the illness likely would be fatal.

Although they dreaded the wait for the sad end and wished that the Katy's life could be sustained, they reluctantly accepted the biblical injunction that "the old order changeth, yielding place to the new." Grieved as most were at the passing of the entity that had given life and significance to their community, the primary concern after the funeral was the unknown future that arrived as a sudden, unwelcome guest.

There was no Winston Churchill to counsel that "this is not the end." But there were residing in the community a special breed of leaders not unlike the promoters who had built the Katy — and Denison — in the beginning. They saw that there was a life after Katy — that the railroad's demise was only "the end of the beginning."

That Denison was not to be "just a railroad town" was perceived when Katy's baby was still an infant. The building of the first plant to ship refrigerated beef and the construction of a giant cotton compress in the 1870's indicate that the town has had innovative leadership from the beginning. Every successful city has been blessed with prophets — promoters with the vision to try something new and different. The building of the Katy itself was such a project, and the heritage of that special breed of pioneers is evident in the leadership of Denison today.

The willingness to experiment — to try something novel — doesn't always succeed. The idea of transforming Main Street into a beautiful shopping mall was laudable. When it failed to live up to expectations, planners responded by restoring the unique serpentine to something akin to the original street. As this is written, the mayor and City Council, the Chamber of Commerce and other groups are hard at work on other plans designed to make this central thoroughfare once again the city's heart.

Although one hears the train blow only rarely in Denison these days, the city is beginning to recognize the fact that it has some assets that cannot be found in very many other places. Hopefully, plans are afoot to capitalize on them.

Birthplace of a President

Only forty spots in the U.S. can make such a claim. In Texas only Johnson City and Denison have that honor.

Although Sam Rayburn's home was Bonham, Denison claimed him, too. The man who was Speaker of the House of Representatives longer than any other individual in history is photographed in his Washington office not long before his death in 1961.

— *Photo courtesy H. C. Dulaney, Sam Rayburn Library*

The white frame house where Dwight D. Eisenhower was born is expected to become an even greater tourist attraction during the coming years.

In 1945, when Denison staged a gala celebration honoring the Katy Railroad on its 75th anniversary, the road turned one of its steam engines into a near replica of the diamond-stacked wood-burner that had brought the first train into Texas on December 25, 1872. The locomotive was used in the celebration and at other points on the system before it and the 1870-model train it pulled were presented to the National Museum of Transport in St. Louis.

The white frame house on West Day, where Dwight D. Eisenhower was born on October 14, 1890, is a site thousands of Americans would like to visit. Hundreds already do. As efforts are made to beautify the surrounding area, provide ample parking and erect good directional signs, this humble home can become a major visitor attraction for Texomaland.

Vineyards to Which the World Owes a Debt

It has been said that wine is a noble, generous liquor, and we should be humbly thankful for it. Denison is. It was there that Thomas Volney Munson, still regarded as probably the greatest viticulturist who ever lived, planted his famous vineyards. He is the reason that every French wine traces its ancestry to the vines he grew on the banks of the Red River and at his home on South Mirick Avenue.

Munson was given the French Legion of Honor — only the second American ever to receive it — for using stock from his Denison grapes to graft the vineyards of France and save them from destruction by disease. (Thomas Jefferson was the first to be so honored by the French.) Munson's

This is the home and vineyards where Thomas Volney Munson experimented with the grapes that made him one of the world's renowned viticulturists. The home still stands in south Denison.

— *Photo by Claud Easterly*

One of the most historic homes still standing in Denison is that of J. B. McDougall, who built an opera house, a hotel at the depot, a bank, and ran a laundry. His stepson was George Moulton, "father of the Denison Dam." The home has been restored in recent years.

— *Claud Easterly photo*

work is known to every winery around the world today, and thousands of wine fanciers would welcome the opportunity to see the city where it all happened and visit the vineyards that now are being restored.

The T. V. Munson Foundation and Museum on the grounds of Grayson County College could become a foremost tourist attraction in Denison's future. It's the only place in the world where those interested in viticulture and wine-making can learn first-hand how Texas grapes served France's most important industry.

Denison — Still a Railroad Town

This city may have lost most of its railroads, but it hasn't lost the heritage of the high iron. There are a quarter of a million organized railroad buffs in the nation who still think of Denison as Katy's baby.

Civic leaders are aware of this and are signaling that "the tracks ahead" will include trains. A Railroad Museum already is in operation at Union Station, and plans for expansion are going on. One day in the future, operable locomotives and a variety of railroad passenger cars may be visited on the tracks at the famous old depot.

If suitable equipment can be found, there is talk of operating an excursion train that would serve dinner and drinks as it traveled between Denison and some nearby point.

As pointed out in an earlier chapter, Denison has all but ignored the fact that it was the place where, on March 10, 1873, the entire nation was joined by rail for the first time. This is a significant event in U.S. and railroad history, and work has

Union Station as it appeared in 1946, when as many as eighteen passenger trains daily served Denison.
— Collection of C. J. McManus

started to get an official historical marker erected on the site south of the Union Station on Main Street. Also, there has been some discussion about an annual observance of this historic occasion.

Another point of interest to rail fans and historians is the spot at 300 E. Johnson Street, where the Atlantic and Texas Refrigerating Co. plant was located. An historical marker there honors Joseph G. McCoy, the man responsible for the famed Chisholm Trail, whose story is related elsewhere in this book. In 1991, the McCoy marker and the historic site are virtually hidden by undergrowth and debris, making it undesirable as a place to be included on an historic tour. This is unfortunate because McCoy, who is credited with saving the cattle industry for Texas, is an important figure in the development of both Texas and the nation.

This historical plaque on East Johnson Street marks the site where Joseph G. McCoy and T. L. Rankin built the plant to slaughter and ship beef by refrigerator cars to eastern markets.

— Photo by Claud Easterly

Medical Center

In recent years, Denison has become the focus of first-rate health care for North Texas and southern Oklahoma. Its Texoma Medical Center is one of the finest facilities of its kind in the nation for a city of this size.

Planners want to do even more in this area. They hope to enlarge Denison's reputation not only for its quality medicine but also as a wellness center. These attributes, plus its excellent climate, already have made Denison a growing choice for retired persons. Early in 1991, plans were announced for a health-related development near Texoma Medical Center that would include a retirement community, condominiums, apartments, a nursery, a hotel or motel, doctors' offices, a rehabilitation center and other amenities.

New Industry

Katy's baby may have lost its parent railroad's offices, shops and yards, but the tracks purchased by the Union Pacific are still in place. Denison may not see as many daily trains as it once did, but it still has direct rail connections with every part of the United States. This makes it especially attractive to new businesses.

Because it is a transportation hub, offers a good labor supply and has good weather, Denison is an ideal location for industry. It is at the north end of an industrial corridor that extends through Dallas, Waco, Austin and San Antonio. It is near enough to the Dallas/Fort Worth International Airport to make travel by air easy. The Denison-Sherman metroplex provides the kind of cultural, entertainment and shopping facilities usually found in much larger cities.

Recreation and Tourism

Lake Texoma, with its excellent marinas and fishing, is a magnet both for tourists and businesses. An estimated eleven million visit the huge lake in a given year, making it one of the nation's most popular recreation areas. Whereas hundreds of travelers used to pass through Denison daily on passenger trains, now thousands of cars drive through the city's heart on U.S. 75. And hundreds pause for overnight stays or complete vacations.

New Life for Main Street?

Even the most optimistic don't expect Main ever to become the central shopping district again. The malls along the highway between Denison and Sherman are easy to access, offer unlimited free parking and a variety of retail establishments, restaurants and theaters in a compact area.

Nevertheless Main Street is coming back, but in a somewhat different guise. The big department stores are gone. So are the theaters (except for the Rialto, which may be restored). Small specialty shops are taking the place of these businesses and more are likely to join them, or so planners believe.

Meanwhile, as indicated in an earlier chapter, far-seeing individuals like Joe and Louis Pollaro are dreaming of turning Main into a theme street that would attract specialty businesses while offering entertainment and relaxation for tourists. Their plan would start with the now closed Denison High School building on the west and extend to the vacant but historic Traveler's Hotel on the east. In between would be a thoroughfare that looked like it did forty years ago.

All of these ideas, and many more, are being explored by the City Council, Chamber of Commerce committees, task forces of citizens and by individuals with innovative ideas. Some of their work is beginning to be evident in events such as craft shows on the street, etc. Other projects are in the exploration stage.

What will be the result of all of this activity remains to be seen. But because Denison's leaders always have been those willing to take a chance, one can be sure that those responsible for the future of Katy's baby will, in the words of Winston Churchill, provide an "end of the beginning" that will insure the continued growth and prosperity of the city they are proud to call home.

The Traveler's Hotel has been a Main Street landmark for decades.
— *Chamber of Commerce*

Bibliography

Acheson, Dr. Alex W. Interview with author, 1932.

Allen, Ruth. *The Great Southwest Strike.* Austin: University of Texas Bureau of Research in the Social Sciences, 1942.

Anderson, Ed H. *History and Business Guide of Sherman and Grayson County, Texas.* 1947.

Bright, Ray. *Legends of the Red River Valley.* San Antonio: The Naylor Co., 1991.

Burton, Art. *Black, Red and Deadly.* Austin: Eakin Press, 1991.

Coffin, A. H. Interview with author, 1936.

Denison *Daily News* files, 1872–1877.

The Denison Guide, American Guide Series. Denison Chamber of Commerce: Federal Writers Project, 1939.

Denison *Herald* Katy Railroad 75th Anniversary Edition, 1945.

Handbook of Texas. Vols. I, II. Austin: Texas State Historical Association, 1952. Vol. III, 1974.

History of Grayson County Texas. Produced by Grayson County Frontier Village, Inc. Winston-Salem, North Carolina: Hunter Publishing Co., 1979.

Joseph, Donald, *Ten Million Acres: The Life of William B. Munson.* Denison: Privately printed, 1946.

Landrum, Graham, and Allan Smith. *An Illustrated History of Grayson County.* Fort Worth: Historical Publications, 1960.

Lowe, Harlan. *A Short History of Denison, Texas, 1873–1900.* Unpublished thesis, 1950.

Maguire, Jack. *A Short History of Denison, Texas.* Denison: The F. W. Miller Company, 1938.

——— "Why There's a Taste of Texas in French Wine." *Southwest Airlines Magazine,* August, 1975.

——— "The Last War Between the States," *Southwest Airlines Magazine,* June 1976.

Masterson, V. V. *The Katy and the Great Southwest.* Norman: University of Oklahoma Press, 1952.

Read, S. G. *A History of Texas Railroads.* Houston: The St. Clair Publishing Co., 1941.

Tobin, Pat H. Interview with author, 1932.

Various city directories by different publishers from 1873 to present.

Index